THE L.A.
DIARIES

BY THE SAME AUTHOR

Lucky Town

The Second Story Theatre

Final Performance

Hot Wire

THE L.A. DIARIES

James Brown

BLOOMSBURY

First published in Great Britain 2004
This paperback edition published 2005

Copyright © 2003 by James Brown

The moral right of the author has been asserted

Bloomsbury Publishing plc, 38 Soho Square, London W1D 3HB

ISBN 0 7475 7466 9

10 9 8 7 6 5 4 3 2 1

All papers used by Bloomsbury Publishing are natural,
recyclable products made from wood grown in well-managed forests.
The manufacturing processes conform to the
environmental regulations of the country of origin.

Printed by Clays Ltd, St Ives plc

www.bloomsbury.com/jamesbrown

In memory of my sister,
Marilyn, and my brother, Barry

CONTENTS

Of this memoir, three pieces appeared in the *Los Angeles Times Magazine:* "My Papa's Waltz," "On Selling a Novel to Hollywood," and "Fire," under the title "A Taste of What Falls from the Sky." "Fire" was also published, in different form, in the *New England Review.* "Daily Rushes" was published in the *Denver Quarterly* and "The Facts" appeared in the *Santa Monica Review.*

The author wishes to thank the editors of these publications and to express gratitude for the generous support received from the National Endowment for the Arts.

FIRE

inter is the season of the arsonist in Southern California. The manzanita and chaparral are dry and brittle and the Santa Ana winds have begun to blow. They move at gale force. They cross the arid Mojave and whip through the canyons of the San Bernardino Mountains, through the live oak and the pines, the ponderosa, the sugar and coulter, white fir and incense cedar. I know these names because I live in these mountains, eighty miles east of the sprawl of Los Angeles, and I worry when the winds come. I worry about the possibility of fire. I know he's out there, the arsonist. I know he's waiting, like me, for a day of opportunity very much like this.

I've seen the Santa Anas uproot trees. I've seen them strip

roofing from houses and shatter windows. I've seen them topple big rigs, and once, along the same freeway I'm traveling now, I saw a stop sign flying through the sky. I keep a firm hold on the wheel. The winds hit in sharp gusts and can blow you clean over the line. You have to be ready. You have to hang on tight and keep your eyes on the road.

Traffic moves slowly, carefully. No one's taking any chances, making abrupt lane changes, cutting you off or tailgating. I would like to believe that it's courtesy that dictates our caution, our good manners, except this is Southern California, I grew up here and I know better. Danger or its potential sometimes brings out the best in us, and I wonder, as I reach to turn on the radio, if maybe it would be a good thing if the Santa Anas blew every day all year-round.

From time to time I find myself having to drive into Los Angeles on business, and just the thought of it always fills me with a sense of dread and anxiety. The city has changed and grown immensely since I knew it as a child, and sometimes even the most familiar streets, streets I grew up on, seem barely recognizable. Gated communities have replaced the bungalows and tract homes and the signs in the windows of the shops and stores are in Vietnamese, Korean, Spanish, occasionally Arabic. Where corner markets once stood you'll now find minimalls, and Hollywood landmarks, places like Schwab's and Pandora's Box and the old Brown Derby restaurant, have gone the way of the bulldozer. There are more freeways, too, bigger and wider ones, but the traffic has never been worse.

But it isn't the unfamiliar that makes me anxious. It isn't the traffic or the crowds or the evolving landscape of architecture and ethnicity. I am a fiction writer who doesn't make enough money at it not to have to do something else for a living. So I teach. So I am a professor. And what Hollywood offers me is the chance to escape the classroom and tell stories full-time. Trouble is, I'm not very good at telling stories that pay better and that's what this is about. It's what it has always been about: my driving into Hollywood to talk to producers and executives who like my work but want me to write something more commercial. In this case that less commercial work is my last novel and the screenplay I wrote based on it, a screenplay commissioned by Universal and Amblin, both of whom passed on it when I was done. "I don't know why you ever bothered to write this," an executive tells me, after she finishes reading my script. "It's no movie. It's too real." Now the rights are mine and my agent, who feels differently than the executive, is sending it to other executives and producers in Hollywood. As a sample, he calls it. The idea is not so much to sell the script as it is to sell myself as a scriptwriter. Already I'm looking forward to the end of the day.

The Santa Anas die down as I approach Los Angeles and I ease up on the wheel. I take a deep breath. But I know it's only temporary, this calm. I know better than to let myself relax. That thing called the L.A. River borders the last stretch of the freeway into Burbank, and I look out on it, the dirty water, moving sluggishly through the narrow concrete channel that contains it. Over the rush of the cars I try to imagine it as I was told it used to be, a real river, filled with trout and salmon and lined with sycamores and willows instead of chain-link and barbed wire. But I'm not successful. I think about my brother. I think about my sister. We are children down by that river on a day very much like this with the wind blowing lightly and the smell of fire in the air. I'm nine years old, the youngest, and we're passing a bottle around, a bottle I've stolen from a grocery store nearby. My sister points to the sky.

"Look. *Look*," she says. "Snow."

Only they're ashes. Ashes are falling. Ashes are everywhere, and in the sunlight they appear white, almost translucent. My head is spinning and I laugh. My brother laughs. I can hear us all laughing as we look to the sky, opening our mouths, catching ashes, like snowflakes, until our tongues turn black.

In the rearview mirror I check to see if my eyes are clear. They are, and they should be. I've gone without a drink or a drug for four days, four long miserable days of white-knuckling it, all because I want to look my best, and I like to think I do. I'm clean shaven. My hair is freshly cut and neatly combed and I have on my best oxford shirt and a brand-new pair of Levi's. But for some reason my heart is beating faster than it should and every now and then I can't seem to catch my breath. It's nerves. I'm under pressure. I see today's meetings as an opportunity and I'm keenly aware that the older I get, the less these opportunities will come my way. It's been six years between novels and now with a new one out, and a new agent working hard to set up these meetings, there is renewed interest in my writing. But that interest is always fleeting. I think about stopping at a liquor store but decide against it. Only alcoholics, I tell myself, drink before noon.

Everything, I tell myself, is under control.

My first meeting is at Disney Studios in Burbank and I arrive early enough to smoke a couple of cigarettes and try to collect myself. There are no soundstages at this end of the lot, and except for a gardener gathering up his hoses, I am alone on a path that divides two generations: On the one side are the older offices, the Hollywood bungalows with stucco exteriors and terra-cotta roofs and well-manicured lawns; on the other are the multistoried buildings made of steel and glass. And at the end of this pathway are the executive offices where I soon find myself, on the third floor, seated across the room from a woman maybe twenty-two, twenty-three at the most. I wonder how she came into her position so young and the only scenarios I come up with have to do with her mother or father or some very good friend. This is just like me, though, to think in the negative, and because I'm aware of it I'm able to check myself. I don't know this woman. I shouldn't prejudge. I'm here for a job, if not today or next week then maybe it'll happen for me a year or two down the line, and I need to remember that. I need to keep an open mind.

For a while it's small talk. I tell her about my drive from the San Bernardino Mountains, the wind and the traffic. She tells me about how bad it used to be when she worked for a law firm in downtown L.A. "Now," she says, "I can walk to my job." Her office looks as if she's in the process of moving into it, or out, I can't tell which. There's a stack of pictures, big framed pictures propped against the couch and it's either because she's taken them down or hasn't hung them yet. Same with the bookcases. They're empty and there are boxes and boxes of screenplays all over the place that need to be unpacked or hauled away.

"I enjoyed your script," she says. "But I wouldn't exactly call it Disney material. I mean it's pretty fucking dark."

She seems relaxed and confident and I wonder if at her age I showed that confidence, or if I've ever had it to show. Certainly I don't now. I look through the window behind her. Outside I can see the tops of the trees swaying in the wind and it occurs to me, though I immediately push the thought out of my mind, that maybe I don't belong here. On her desk is a bag of peanuts and every now and then, as we continue to talk, she reaches for one, cracks it open with her teeth and drops the shells on the carpet.

"Are you working on anything new?"

"Another script," I say.

"What about?" she says, popping a peanut into her mouth.

I'm lying. I'm not working on another script, at least not putting words to paper, but then that's what this is all about. To pitch. To sell what you haven't written and probably never will unless you're paid first. I think my idea is commercial.

"It starts out in the desert," I say. "You see this man all by himself in the middle of nowhere. It's toward nightfall and at first you can't tell what he's doing. But he's got a long steel pole and he's jabbing it into the ground. The camera pulls back and we see hundreds of holes all over the desert floor. He's been doing it all day."

"And why's he doing this?"

She asks the question but I'm not so sure that she's interested in the answer. This does little for my confidence.

"He's searching for his daughter," I say. "Checking for soft spots in the ground."

The producer shifts in her seat.

"That's a real cheery opening," she says.

I smile awkwardly. I clear my throat, I push on.

"The next thing we see is a parade of news vans following a sheriff's car into the desert. The killer's in the backseat. Pull over, he says. He points out the window with his cuffs on and that's when we cut away, to the same scene, only now we're watching it on TV. It's a videotape, and the killer's face is frozen on the screen." I pause, waiting for her response, but she just cracks open another peanut and pops it into her mouth. "The father, the guy we saw in the beginning, we're in his living room now. He's slouched in an old lounge chair staring at the TV and all around him are empty beer cans and whiskey bottles and half-eaten plates of food. The poor bastard's been playing the same scene over and over. Hasn't moved from that chair in days."

I pause again for her reaction and she gives me a strange look, as if I might be a little over the edge myself for having thought it up. And in a way, I suppose, she may be right.

"Christ, don't you write anything light?"

"You want light, I got light."

But that's as far as I get.

"To tell you the truth," she says, "we're really not taking on new projects now anyway. But I have a script that could use some work. Maybe you'd like to take a look at it."

Of course I would. What I want is a chance, any sort of chance, and in this case it's a shot at a rewrite of someone else's screenplay, an adaptation of a novel called *Going Blind*, about a college music professor who's slowly losing his sight and tries to hide the fact from his friends and family and colleagues for as long as he can. He can't face what's happening to him, can't admit to the truth, and I think I can understand that. I think it's something I can work on, even with the changes she wants, which are to set the story in high school instead of college and make him a football coach instead of a music professor. My first reaction is that it strains credibility, to make him a football coach. But it's possible, I suppose. Anything is possible when there's money involved, and before I leave her office I'm already working on it, trying to imagine different scenes, different predicaments, trying to imagine myself as a man going blind.

My next meeting isn't for a couple of hours, and I'm back in my car with nothing to do. I think about getting something to eat. I think about getting a cup of coffee. But I'm nervous and jittery and what I really want is something to take the edge off. My sister lives nearby in Studio City and ordinarily, whenever I come into L.A., I drop by and have a couple of drinks with her. Do a line. Or two. Or three. Only these aren't ordinary times. She's quit drinking and using since the death of baby Katherine and I don't feel welcome in her home anymore. Still I want her to be clean and sober. Still I am proud of my sister and I've told her so. That doesn't mean, however, that I have to follow her example. Because I can take it or leave it. I can quit whenever I want. I fumble for my car keys, start the engine and drive into Hollywood to kill some time.

The plan is to hit a bookstore or maybe cruise by one of my old neighborhoods and see how it's changed, or maybe how it hasn't. Our mother moved around a lot when we were growing up and it's hard to go anywhere in this city without bumping into someplace we used to live. An old apartment complex. Some shabby house. I went to fourteen different schools before I reached the ninth grade, and one year, the first year we moved to Los Angeles, my brother, sister and I didn't attend school at all. The area was too rough, our mother said, and she was right. Barry and Marilyn were beat up the first couple of weeks of classes, and I had my share of trouble, too. Until we could afford a better neighborhood, a better school district, our mother thought it best that we ride the year out at home.

But today I don't stick to my plan. I don't go to a bookstore. I don't drive by the old neighborhoods. Instead I make myself a promise: I'll only have one. Just one. I mean it, too. At the time I couldn't mean it more. And of course after the first drink I see no harm in having a second. Or a third. I sit at the far end of the bar, under the Olympia waterfall, and further justify my being here by reading the script to *Going Blind.* At least, I tell myself, I am being constructive while I drink.

It's good, the way the writer has it, from the point of view of a music professor, and the more I read, the less I'm able to imagine it differently. A teacher who is going blind could make himself intimately familiar with the physical layout of his classroom and soon learn to move about it with something close to ease. I can buy that. And certainly he could play his instrument, which in this case happens to be the piano. But a blind football coach? What happens when he steps out onto the field? When he has to call a play, or simply throw the ball? The drinks have begun to take effect and I'm able to see things clearly now, for what they really are: The whole idea is fucking ridiculous, and I feel like a fool for ever having gotten my hopes up. That I hoped at all just goes to show how desperate I am, and I hate to think that the producer saw it in me, that desperateness, although I'm sure that she did. Then I start to think about how she kept cracking peanuts while we talked and dropping the shells on the carpet and how someone would have to clean them up. I bet it won't be her. In fact, I bet she's used to making messes for others to clean up, messes much bigger than peanut shells, and I resent her for it. I resent myself, too, for trying to sell someone a story that I don't believe in and would never write unless I was paid.

So I light another cigarette.

So I order another drink and pretty soon I find myself condemning not only the producer who gave me the script but also the one that I'm scheduled to meet, and never will, because by now I'm too drunk. And by now it's too late. Exactly how long I've been here, I don't know, but when I drink I often lose complete sense of time and this is one of those occasions.

Once I drove halfway across the state to visit my in-laws for Christmas, a good five hundred miles, and I barely remember getting into the car. Suddenly it's eight, nine hours later and I'm there, parked in my in-laws' driveway, listening to the engine tick itself cool. How I made it without getting into a wreck, maybe killing myself or someone else, is something akin to a miracle.

I pick up some change from the bar and head to the pay phone on the wall outside the bathrooms and call my sister. She answers on the second ring.

"Hey, Marilyn," I say.

"Where the hell are you?"

"I'm at a gas station. My fan belt broke."

"Bullshit."

"No bullshit."

"You should be calling your wife," she says, "not me."

There's a long pause. I twist the phone cord around my hand.

"Just tell her I'm on my way, okay?"

"I'm sick of lying for you."

"It's no lie," I say.

"Jimmy," she says. "I can hear the fucking music in the background. You better sober up and get your ass home."

My wife's name is Heidi, and I know I should call her, that I owe her that much, but I don't want to hear it. Her cursing.

Her screaming. I know I've done wrong. I know there's no excuse for getting drunk when you're supposed to be home with your family and I wish knowing this would stop me from doing it. I wish that's all it took. That I could *will* it to happen. But it doesn't work that way, it never has, and in my state of mind, at this particular moment, I can't imagine living without it. The alcohol. The dope. I've been drinking and using since I was nine years old and sometimes I think it's the only thing that gives me any real pleasure. I love the feeling, the rush. That numbing of the brain. That deadening of the senses or the heightening of them on speed. I need that drink. That pill, that fix, to feel better. I need it, sometimes, just to make it through another day.

It's dark out when I finally leave the bar, and the Santa Anas have kicked up again. I'm on Hollywood Boulevard, and even for a weeknight the streets seem abnormally quiet. Few cars are on the road, and the sidewalks, usually crowded with tourists, are strangely empty. The wind is strong and I lower my head and lean into it as I walk, in the opposite direction from where I parked. At the corner there's an old man waiting for the light to change and I ask him for the time. He doesn't seem to hear me. I repeat the question, only louder. That gets him to glance my way but again he doesn't say anything. Maybe he's scared to be out on these streets at night. Maybe he smells the liquor on me and it offends him. I don't know. When the light changes he steps off the curb, holding his jacket closed against his chest and hurries across the street.

I walk on.

My legs are heavy and the lights in the windows of the different shops and stores are blurred. For the first time that night I realize I'm drunk. Too drunk to drive. I need more than coffee to sober up. But I'm in luck. This is Hollywood and whatever you want, whatever you need is always just around the corner or a little farther down the block. Tonight I find it outside a run-down apartment complex on a side street between Vine and Cahuenga. Two Puerto Rican kids are standing on the front steps, and I catch eyes with the smaller one as I walk by. There's a boom box at his feet and the bigger kid is sipping on a can of Olde English "800."

"Anything happening?" I say.

"What you looking for?"

"Rock. Crank. Whatever you got."

"You a cop?"

"I look like a cop?"

"Yeah," the smaller one says, "you look like a fucking cop."

"You look like a fucking cop, too," I say.

But I say it in a good way, because I'm in a good mood. Because I know I'm about to score. Besides it's only protocol: If you're a cop and don't say so when you're asked, that's grounds for entrapment. They know it, I know it, and for fifty dollars they point me to a chink in the apartment wall, just a few feet away, where they've stashed a tiny plastic bag of what proves, surprisingly, to be some very potent dope. For another ten I get a chipped glass pipe that sells new for a couple of bucks but I'm not interested in bargaining. Like Pavlov's dogs, my mouth is suddenly dry, my heart is beating faster and I can almost feel it, the rush, without even firing up.

I plan to get high in my car where there's less chance of being seen, and where I'm out of the wind, but it's parked a few blocks away and I can't wait that long. All the stores on Hollywood Boulevard are closed for the night, and I duck into the alcove of a souvenir shop, drop a rock into the pipe and light up. My back is to the street and at first, when I feel a wave of heat pass over me, I think it's on account of the dope, the rush. That it's just powerful stuff. But then it happens again, an even stronger wave along the back of my neck, and that's when I realize that it's coming from behind me. Turning, I see it: The building directly across the street is immersed in fire. And it's a beautiful sight. Flames seep through the edges of the roof and the big storefront windows glow and pulsate like they're breathing. Burning embers dance across the sky. In the powerful Santa Anas the flames grow fast, and in a matter of seconds they've doubled in size. I look around to see if anyone else is watching but the streets are empty. This makes me nervous. I'm the sole witness to what is most likely the work of an arsonist, and I don't want to be anywhere near here when the police and firefighters arrive, especially in my condition. Ashes rain from the sky, and I begin to walk.

Everything, I tell myself, is under control.

I don't remember the ride home that night any better than I do the time I drove halfway across the state to visit my in-laws for Christmas. That's the nature of a blackout. But I must've stopped off at a liquor store along the way because there's a pint of Canadian Club in my lap. And most of it is empty. It's light out now, and somehow I've managed to navigate my way home. Sixty miles of freeway. Another twenty of winding mountain roads. I'm parked in the driveway outside my house, and the windshield is silver with frost. Exactly how long I've been there, I can't say for sure, but when I wake up I'm shivering from the cold and everything is quiet. The branches on the big pines that surround my house are motionless and there's a certain stillness about the air, a certain calm. The Santa Anas have passed finally and now, lightly at first, it begins to snow.

She will threaten to leave me.

She will tell me over and over that I am a horrible man and I will promise repeatedly, as I always do, repeatedly, never to hurt her and our beautiful children again. I will vow never to drink. I will vow never to use. I will vow, from here on out, to be a responsible man. And I will mean all these things. I will mean each and every one.

Faintly I hear the sound of laughter, and on the hillside in the distance I spot my three little boys. They are bundled up in heavy jackets. They're wearing knit caps and bright-colored scarves and mittens too big for their hands. The snow falls harder. The snow falls faster, and as I start toward the house I watch them spinning round and round, laughing, their mouths open to the sky.

SNAPSHOT

I'm waiting in the car for my mother while she sets fire to an apartment building down the street. I'm five years old. The car is a new Thunderbird with big wide seats that still smell of fresh vinyl, and the street where we are parked is lined with sycamores that have begun to shed their leaves. It is early in the evening. We are in a quiet working-class neighborhood in San Jose, California, fifty miles south of San Francisco along Highway 101, and when my mother returns to the car, slightly out of breath, we drive to Fisherman's Wharf and have shrimp cocktails for dinner.

Afterward we catch a cable car. The rumble of the steel wheels and the jerkiness of the ride scares me but I feel safe with my mother's arm around me. My brother and sister are back in San Jose with our father, and I like it this way, being alone with her. Barry is eleven years old, Marilyn is just nine, and for once I don't have to compete with them for our mother's attention. In the distance, as the cable car reaches the top of Nob Hill, you can see the skyline lit up with the lights from all the different office buildings. You can see the fog rolling in off the bay, unfurling across the city.

My mother shivers and holds me tighter.

"I want to buy you a present," she says.

"What for?"

"Just because," she says.

We get off at the end of the line and walk down Market Street, pausing every now and then to look through the windows of the different shops and stores. I like the cutlery shop with all its knives laid out in perfect rows. Bowies and stilettos. Fat butcher knives. Hunting knives, daggers and swords. The chromed and steel blades shine under the glare of the bright lights. I stare and stare until my mother takes my hand.

"C'mon," she says, pulling me along. "You're too young for a knife."

We head down the block, her high heels clicking against the pavement. When we come to an army surplus she stops and asks me if I want to go in. I tell her that I do. It smells good inside, musty and damp, and for a while my mother lets me wander the aisles by myself. They have old army helmets. They have old G.I. canteens. They have field jackets, German parkas, empty ammunition cans, scalpels and tweezers, duffel bags and rucksacks. The list goes on.

I'm looking at a portable foxhole shovel with a folding blade when my mother finds me. It unfolds easily enough but now I'm having trouble breaking it back down, like I found it.

"The store is closing," my mother says. "Hurry and pick something out."

It's between the foxhole shovel and one of the old army helmets, and I choose the foxhole shovel in part because I'm curious as to how it breaks down, which I feel I'm just on the verge of figuring out, and in part because I can imagine myself digging a deep hole with it in our backyard. Maybe, if I dug wide enough, I could turn it into an underground clubhouse. Maybe, if I covered the top with leaves and branches, I could make a trap for my brother and sister. With a good shovel, there are all kinds of possibilities. With a helmet, all you can do is wear it, and of course none of them fit. I give the shovel to my mother and she pays the cashier.

On our way back to the cable cars we encounter a man sprawled out on the sidewalk, one hand hanging limply over the curb, the other clutching a thin green bottle to his chest. I think he could be dead, or badly injured, and I want to stop. I want to see if there's anything we should do to help. But my mother knows different. She grew up poor in Chicago and has witnessed these kinds of things all her life.

She squeezes my hand. "Don't worry," she says. "He's okay. He's just a drunk."

We make a wide arc around him. We continue down the block but I keep glancing over my shoulder at him. He doesn't look okay to me, not at all. My mother hurries me along, and I wonder, as I turn my back to the man, what exactly a drunk is and why it is that he doesn't deserve our concern.

We spend the night at the Travel Lodge on Beach Street. There's only one bed in the room but it's large enough for both of us, and I remember lying beside my mother in the dark, listening to the cars passing on the street outside the window. She has her back to me. I remember her gentle, even breathing and the warmth of her skin against mine. I don't think she is sleeping. Even at that early age I sense that something is wrong, terribly wrong, and for a long while I also remain awake. The headlights from the passing cars outside make shadows on the ceiling, and I watch them, the different patterns, how they bend and disappear.

In the morning we have breakfast at the coffee shop next to our motel. The counter is full of men reading the newspaper, smoking cigarettes and drinking coffee. We sit in a booth near the back. My mother looks tired, in no mood for the men at the counter who keep glancing her way. She dips the corner of her napkin into a glass of ice water on the table.

"Hold still," she says.

Leaning toward me, she draws the wet part of the napkin along my cheek. The water is cold. I wince and pull away. "How you get so dirty," she says, "I'll never know." The waitress brings her coffee, and afterward, when we've ordered and eaten our breakfast, we return to the car in the parking lot of the motel.

For most of the ride home that morning we say little. It's still foggy out and she is concentrating on the road. Highway 101 runs parallel to San Francisco Bay, and I look out over the gray choppy waters as we drive. We pass Candlestick Park, where our father once took us to watch the Shriners' all-star game. We pass the San Francisco airport. We pass through the sprawling suburbs of Brisbane, Burlingame and Palo Alto and then we are back, moving along the familiar streets of San Jose where again, while we are stopped for a red light, I catch a couple of men staring at my mother. They're standing at the bus stop on the corner, and one of them whistles. I give him a dirty look. The other guy smiles at me. My mother ignores them both, and when the light changes we drive on. I'm too young to realize why men stare at my mother so much but I'll understand when I'm older and look at some old snapshots of her.

I am looking at one now, as I write this.

It is pinned to the wall in front of me, and in it my mother, brother, sister and I are standing in front of an older Buick Special. We are squinting against the glare of the sun, and in the background you can see the wide expanse of the Pacific. I look closer at the photograph. My mother's hair is cut short, like a boy's, and she is wearing a white sleeveless sweater, a tight skirt, and sandals. One of her legs is posed ahead of her. Her hands are laced behind her back, and she's leaning against the fender, smiling pleasingly into the camera.

This house is an achievement for our father, a building con-tractor with an eleventh-grade education, and our mother, a secretary and real estate agent who dropped out in junior high. It is Spanish style, painted white with brown trimming, the roof terra-cotta. The front lawn is neatly manicured. Inside there are three bedrooms, two baths, a den and an office. Through hard work, scrimping and saving, they have also ac-quired six other houses in San Jose. They buy them run-down, fix them up, then sell or rent them out. They are doing well. Marilyn and Barry attend private schools and take piano and dance lessons. We have a baby-sitter, a beautiful Mexican woman a few years older than our mother, a woman who reads to me, who makes us breakfast, makes our beds, does our laun-dry, shops for us and keeps our house clean.

I share a room with my brother, and when I get home that

morning I find him stretched out across his bed reading. He's always reading, it seems. Big fat books. By eleven Barry has skipped two grades. He can speak French and Spanish and his IQ tests out at 170, genius level. Someday he wants to be a movie star. Already he's had two small roles in Equity theater in San Francisco and a walk-on in the movie *All's Fair in Love and War.* This is our mother's idea, for Barry to act, though he's taken to it as if it were his own. He is the classic overachiever, ambitious, driven to please. As a child Barry is bone-thin, sickly and pale from lack of sun and exercise. Fun, or play as other children know it, is not an important part of his life.

My brother is reading *Profiles in Courage.* John F. Kennedy has recently been elected president, and Barry is a big Kennedy fan. Usually he ignores me when he's reading, usually he ignores me in general, but this morning is different. He puts the book down and looks at me when I come into the room. I'm carrying the foxhole shovel.

"Where did you and Mom go last night?"

"San Francisco."

"Why'd she take you?"

"I don't know," I say. "She just told me to come."

"The fight wasn't that big a deal. They've had a lot worse."

"She said she had to get away from him," I say.

He shakes his head. He picks up the book and begins to read again.

"I don't see why," he says. "She was doing all the yelling."

My brother and I share bunk beds. He has the lower half. I have the top. I climb up to my bed and sit Indian-style. The foxhole shovel unscrews at the base of the handle so that the blade can drop up or down, and I play with it for a while, screwing and unscrewing it. The threads are rusty and make a grating noise. I hear my brother sigh. I hear him slap his book shut and leave the room.

Maybe he worries about losing her for good. Maybe he knows that you can only fight so long before you just wear out and give up. I can't say. I can't say much about a lot of things that happened, or didn't happen, between my mother and father. But he is fourteen years older than her and less volatile, less willing to meet her head-on. If he is angry about her taking me and running off to San Francisco, he doesn't show it when he gets home from work that night. In fact, they both act as if nothing has happened. She makes dinner. He mixes drinks. They get along perfectly. At this point only our mother knows what she has done, and it surprises me, when I think about it, how calmly she is able to conduct herself that night.

There is a story about the fire in the local newspaper the next day. An old woman who lived on the top floor of the apartment died of smoke inhalation. And another old woman, who lived in the complex next door, is quoted as saying that she saw someone, a younger woman, leave the laundry room and hurry down the street and into a new Thunderbird shortly before the fire broke out. That in itself doesn't seem like evidence enough to single someone out, let alone make an arrest, but there are details that the newspaper doesn't print, details that will surface in court. They come for our mother a few nights later while Barry, Marilyn and I are lying on the living room floor. All the lights are out and it's dark except for the gray-white flicker of the television. We are watching *House of Wax.* Our father isn't home from work yet, or maybe he's stopped off at a bar along the way, but our mother is there, seated on the armchair behind us. She is the first to notice them—the patrol car, its headlamps off and motor dead—roll quietly down the driveway.

"Get up," she says. "Hurry."

She herds us behind the couch. We crouch there, waiting. Barry is the boldest.

"What's going on?" he asks.

"Quiet."

"Mom?"

The beam of a flashlight shines through the living room window and lands on the wall behind us. My mother has her arm around me. She is wearing a pale blue nightgown and one strap has slipped off her shoulder. I can smell her sweat. I can hear her shallow breathing. Then the doorbell rings. Another beam from a flashlight glances across the ceiling and we hear the footsteps of one of the men on our front porch. His voice is flat, monotone.

"Mrs. Brown," he shouts. "Mrs. Brown. This is the sheriff of Santa Clara County."

From around the edge of the couch I can see the television. It's near the end of the movie. The heroine is cornered by Vincent Price, the curator of the museum, and she pounds at his face. Only it's a mask, and it cracks away, in chunks, like porcelain. The face behind it has been hideously disfigured by fire, the skin molten and hardened.

They do not take her that night. They do not take her the next. But they will take her soon enough with her attorney, Mr. Menken, negotiating the terms of her surrender. Before then she will have to tell our father about the charges, and she will deny them, and he will believe her because he needs to believe, because he loves her.

"I was with Jimmy," she tells him. "We went to San Francisco."

What she does not tell him is that they are bankrupt. That over the last year she has been forging his name and selling and mortgaging the properties they own. She does this to cover the loss of some poor investments she made without our father's knowledge. This includes the mortgaging of our own house, though it does nothing to explain why she would burn down an apartment complex they do not own. Those are two things that none of us, except maybe our mother, will ever understand.

The Jose Theater in downtown San Jose is playing *The Errand Boy* with Jerry Lewis. The box office opens at eleven forty-five. The first showing begins at noon. This is Saturday morning, and our father drops us off early, a few minutes before the box office opens. He gives Barry the money for our tickets. He tells him to keep an eye on me. He tells Marilyn the same.

"Stay together," he says. "Don't let Jimmy out of your sight, not for a second. I'll pick you up when the movie's over."

I am expecting Barry to protest, to speak out on our behalf. We do not want to see *The Errand Boy*. We do not want to see any movie because we know why he is doing this and it isn't right. He has told us nothing. We have overheard nothing. Still we know things. We know them intuitively, and we resent him for it, for the silence that lies.

It's the way our father looks at him. It's how that look lingers, and as Barry shuts the car door and turns away, without a word, I begin to suspect that he's a part of it, this conspiracy, this lie. I begin to suspect that as the oldest he has been taken aside, sworn to secrecy and told things that Marilyn and I are supposedly too young to understand. Our father drives off. We start for the box office. Barry grabs my hand, but I am too old to hold hands, and I pull away.

"Hey," he says, "what's the matter with you?"

"Nothing," I say.

"You don't act like it."

"Leave him alone," Marilyn says. "If he doesn't want to hold hands, he doesn't want to hold hands. Don't force him."

Ordinarily she sides with Barry. She is his biggest admirer, his greatest ally in a family divided by favorites. But today, on this small matter, Marilyn sides with me. We stand together in line at the box office. We sit together inside the theater and share a box of popcorn that she buys with her own money. I feel privileged, special for her attention. My sister is a shy, soft-spoken girl and I like that about her.

"Are you all right?" she asks. "You okay?"

I don't say anything. But in the darkness of the theater, I reach for her hand.

On-screen Jerry Lewis is screaming and making grotesque, distorted faces. The audience laughs, and we laugh with them, but for us it's not real. None of this is real. None of this is happening. If you just don't think about it, everything will be fine, and when our father picks us up later that afternoon and drives us home she will be there, as she always is, making dinner maybe, maybe talking on the phone. But she will be there. I will tell her about the movie. I will say that it was really funny.

Really crazy. And then I will go out to the backyard and dig a hole with the shovel she bought me.

I will dig for hours while our father sits alone at the kitchen table and drinks. Marilyn will lock herself in her room and cry. Barry will open another book. The hole will grow. If I dig long enough, if I dig deep enough, she will call me in for dinner. I will dig until the sky is dark.

The old woman who allegedly saw my mother leave the laundry room of the apartment complex and drive off in a new Thunderbird shortly before the fire broke out is found to have something less than 20/20 vision. She also takes several prescription medications that can adversely affect judgment and motor skills. Her age, of course, is another strike, and in the end the prosecutors for the State of California determine that she is not a credible witness. Because there are no other witnesses, and because there is no apparent motive for our mother to have started the fire, the original charges of arson and second-degree murder are dropped. Instead they prosecute and convict her for what they can prove: tax evasion. For several years running our mother knowingly failed to report the income from the sale and mortgaging of the properties she and our father owned. Her punishment is two years at the Center for Women in Alviso, California, and restitution to the federal and state governments, which cannot be paid because she has bankrupted us.

In her psychiatric evaluation she is diagnosed with a serious mental disorder, and the judge offers to reduce her sentence if she will serve her time in a state psychiatric hospital. In doing so he would allow her to return home once a month to visit her husband and children. But to accept the offer is to accept the diagnosis and our mother refuses to be stigmatized. Maybe it's about pride. Maybe it's about denial. The problem, if there is one, doesn't exist if you don't acknowledge it, and the choice she makes is a painful one.

In the months to come we are evicted from the home we grew up in. The Thunderbird is repossessed. Our father files for bankruptcy and we move into a run-down, one-bedroom apartment on the poor side of town not far from where our former babysitter lives. At school word leaks out and my brother, my sister and I are teased and ridiculed. "Your mother is in prison," they say. "Your mother is a murderer." In defense Barry retreats further into his books. Marilyn finds solace in God at the Lutheran church and dreams of one day becoming a missionary. I fight. And I do it often. I am a problem for the teachers. I am six years old now, in the first grade, and I am considered a threat to other students. The school psychologist says that I am emotionally disturbed and recommends that I be placed in the special education program. The kids are tougher there, and I learn more. To always throw the first punch. To always hurt others before they hurt you, and to hurt them good, so they will remember.

I am suspended often.

Usually it is for fighting but one time it is because I am not properly bathed and dressed. My father leaves for the construction site in the morning before I'm out of bed. My brother and sister are also on different schedules and leave for school earlier than I do. I don't know who is at fault, except myself, but then you can't expect much from a boy at this age. He doesn't worry about washing his face or brushing his teeth. He doesn't think about combing his hair. And the clothes he wears, the ones he wore playing in the dirt the day before, and the day before that, they're as good as any.

Our father won't accept welfare, his pride doesn't permit it, though every week several bags of groceries mysteriously appear on our doorstep. Once I came home and found a bike in the hallway with a note with my name on it taped to the handlebars. It's no secret, we know our benefactor, but she prefers to remain anonymous, and of course we go along with it. Of course we are appreciative, and in my hazy memory these gifts, this sense of goodwill, are connected with a more significant event that occurs around this time—one night, in our apartment, as it's getting on toward dinner.

Marilyn is at the stove boiling water for spaghetti. Barry is sitting at the kitchen table looking out the window. Our apartment is on the second floor, and from that window you can see down into the carports.

33

"C'mere," he says.

"What for?"

"Just c'mere."

He is talking to Marilyn but it's the sound of his voice that gets me up off the floor. I am in the living room watching TV, and when I come into the kitchen I find them both looking out the window. In the shadow of the light in the carports below, where he must believe that they can't be seen, our father is holding our former baby-sitter. "We can't tell Mom. We can't tell anyone," Barry says. "Not a soul. I just thought you guys should know." She has her arms wrapped around our father's neck. His hands are clasped together behind the small of her back. Aileen is her name, she is our benefactor, and we watch them as they kiss. We watch them that night, and others, in the shadow of the light in the carports below.

I am in my father's work truck, sitting on my hands to keep them warm. The heater is broken, and this is winter. It is several days before Christmas and he is taking me to visit my mother, who I have not seen in almost thirteen months. For the occasion my hair is freshly cut, I am dressed in slacks, Hush Puppies and a white button-down shirt that my sister ironed for me shortly before we left. On the seat beside me is the Christmas stocking that I made for my mother at school, of red crepe paper, white yarn and silver glitter for snow. My father is sullen as he drives. His eyes rarely stray from the road. He talks little. The Center for Women is in the neighboring town of Alviso, about twenty miles south of San Jose, but it seems much farther.

My brother and sister are not taking this trip, and they never will. Though our father visits her often, until now she has not wanted to see any of her children, or rather she has not wanted any of her children to see her under these circumstances. Probably I am the exception because I am younger—too young, they must think, to be affected, to understand. And maybe they are right. At my age I have little notion of the indignities of prison life. I am not likely to judge her. I am not likely to ask the sort of questions that her older children might.

In the visiting room there is a long counter divided by a sheet of thick glass with wire running through it. I sit on my father's lap in a steel fold-out chair. My mother sits across from us on the other side in the same kind of chair, and she is thinner than I remembered, wearing a shapeless green smock. Her hair is cut short like a boy's. Her fingernails are not painted, and she is without her makeup, no dark eyeliner, no lipstick or blush. You talk through phone receivers, only there isn't any phone. As a child I find this strange.

"How's my little Jimmy?" she says.

"Fine," I say.

"You look so handsome," she says. "All dressed up. How do you like school? You started first grade this year."

"It's okay."

"Just okay?"

I hold up the present I made her.

"This is for you," I say.

"It's beautiful," she says. "Did you get my present yet?"

It came in the mail a few days earlier, and on the back of the package she wrote: *Don't open until Christmas.* Inside I found a handkerchief with a Viking ship embroidered across it. My name is stitched in the corner in flowing red letters.

"Yeah," I tell her. "I got it."

"Don't open it until Christmas."

"I won't."

"Promise?"

"Promise," I say.

She smiles. I smile back. We talk a while longer. She wants to know about Barry and Marilyn, if everything is all right, if we're all getting along, and soon, after a lull in the conversation, she tells me to put my father on.

"I love you, baby," she says. "I love you."

There's a guard at the door on my mother's side of the counter, standing with her hands behind her back. There's a guard at the door on our side of the counter, too, and when the visit is over, when our time has run out, my father gives her the crepe-paper stocking to pass along to my mother. I don't know exactly what happens to her after that. Or if seeing me has anything to do with it. But somewhere between Alviso and San Jose, while my father and I drive home in silence, my mother is placed in solitary confinement.

The story, as I heard from my father years later, goes something like this: She returns to her cell after we leave and all is as usual. Then her cellmate says something, or maybe she just looks at her the wrong way. I don't know. I wasn't there and my mother never liked to talk about it. But I'm not surprised. I know what she's capable of if provoked, and fortunately her actions didn't result in a longer sentence. From what I understand they got into it good and she bit the woman's ear off. Clean through. To where the flesh joins the skull.

On the six o'clock news you see the motorcade moving slowly along a wide sunlit street in downtown Dallas. We are watching this, Barry, Marilyn and I, while our mother and father rage in the kitchen about his affair. She has been home now for several days, and as we watch the scene unfold on TV we try to block them out. It is old news by a week or better but the broadcasters continue to play it nightly: President Kennedy and his wife, Jackie, are riding in the backseat of a black Lincoln convertible. They are waving to the crowds on the sidewalks when he leans toward his wife as if he wants to whisper something in her ear and the side of his face explodes. Then you see Jackie rise from her seat. At first it looks as if she's trying to climb out of the car, that she's afraid for her own life. But really all she's concerned about is gathering up the pieces of her husband that landed on the back of the trunk. Her impulse is to put him back together. Of course that's impossible but it doesn't mean that there isn't beauty in the moment, in her desperateness to salvage what can't be saved.

In the kitchen our parents continue to rage. They are drinking as they argue and the drinking only makes them more volatile. "It's over," she says. "I'm taking the kids and we're going to Los Angeles where Barry can make something of himself. There's nothing you can do about it," she says. "You lost your rights when you fucked that woman." I don't remember our father's response, though I'm sure he fought back. I know he loved us. But I also know about the insidiousness of guilt, how it distorts judgment and weakens your resolve. One of the last memories I have of that night is of our mother later passed out on the couch. The rest is pretty much a blur. But the next day our father makes a deal to remodel someone's kitchen in exchange for an older Buick Special. That's the car in the snapshot I keep pinned on my wall, the one showing my brother and sister and me squinting against the glare of the sun. In the background you can see the wide expanse of the Pacific. My sister is wearing a funny straw hat with a flower in the band.

My mother's hair is cut short, like a boy's, since it hasn't had time to grow out yet, and her lips are painted bright red. She is smiling pleasingly into the camera. My pants are rolled up to the knees because I've been in the water, and if I look closely I can make out faint trails of sand on my legs.

The photograph is taken at Pismo Beach when we pull off Highway 101, about halfway between San Jose and our destination. Sometimes, when I look at it, I imagine them as strangers: All I see are three children and a woman who could be their mother. I like to think that their father is there somewhere, maybe snapping the picture, that this is just another family on vacation. They are standing against the background of the ocean and they look small, almost fragile. It's another boy, the one with his pants rolled up to the knees. It's someone else's mother. It's someone else's brother, someone else's sister wearing the funny straw hat with the flower in the band, and their story, whatever happens to them, bears no connection to my own.

DAILY RUSHES

I'm driving into Los Angeles again for another important meeting. Depending on traffic, Caltrans roadwork or wrecks, the trip takes anywhere from ninety minutes to three hours one way. It's rarely less even if I speed, and occasionally it's more. There have been days when all five lanes on the San Bernardino Freeway have literally come to a complete, seemingly final stop, and I've shut off the engine, climbed out of my car and smoked a cigarette between the dividing barriers. I've learned to be patient. I've learned to accept these delays as inevitable, as necessary, as something as basic to Southern California as its beaches, its earthquakes and its random drive-by shootings.

But the traffic is light this morning, no Sig-Alerts or Cal-trans roadwork to back it up, and I get to Universal Studios a full hour early. This is a mistake. Because now I'm left with too much time to get nervous, and I'm already nervous. I want a drink but I'm not going to take one, at least not until this is over, and then it will be as a reward for having survived the day. I pull into the driveway and stop at the guard booth.

"I'm here for a meeting," I say.

I give him my name. I give him the executive's name and the guard checks his ledger. For a moment I worry that I might not be on the list. The executive's assistant could've forgotten to phone down my pass. Or maybe we got our dates mixed up. Anything could happen.

"What time?" he says.

"Ten thirty," I say.

He continues to scan the ledger, and now I'm feeling like some sort of impostor, that he thinks I'm trying to pull a fast one on him. I could be a desperate, overzealous actor attempting to lie my way into a casting office. I could be a crazed fan. Or an autograph hound. That I'm driving an older Toyota doesn't help matters. Finally the guard comes up with my pass.

"You're a little early," he says.

And before I can explain about my long drive from the mountains of San Bernardino and the need to anticipate the unexpected, like wrecks or traffic or Caltrans problems, the gate rises and he waves me through. I doubt if he wanted to hear my story anyway. I know I wouldn't have if I were him.

My meeting with the executive is in the Black Tower, a skyscraper of steel and glass, and to kill time I buy myself a cup of coffee, smoke four or five cigarettes, and walk in circles around the studio commissary.

Through a window in the waiting room on the tenth floor of the Black Tower I look out over the green rolling hills of Forest Lawn where my brother is buried. He was twenty-seven and alcoholic when he ended his life, and at this moment, in this place and time, I see myself in him, sitting here, waiting to meet with an executive. I imagine he once occupied this same space, if not this exact office then another in the building, and I imagine he felt as I do now. Anxious. In need of a drink. Maybe, like me, he questioned why he was here, if this was what he really wanted. If he belonged. Maybe, like me, he was both repelled and attracted to a business that is at least in part responsible for his destruction.

On a bookshelf nearby are rows and rows of screenplays, the pages of each loosely bound with brass brads. The titles are written in black felt pen along the spines. Some of the names I recognize. I've seen them on the big screen. Others, if they've been made, I've never heard of. Generally a script averages a hundred and twenty pages, but I've been told that the ideal

length is about a hundred, and if you can whittle it down to
ninety, that's even better. Pages are time. Time is money. Expo-
sition, all those words, all that ink on the page, or "black shit,"
as a producer I once met referred to it, ought to be kept to a
minimum.

"You want a fast read," he said. "The story has to move like
a rocket. All the pieces have to fit, exactly, down to the minute.
Down to the dollar."

And I listen.

Because I'm concerned about these things, the pieces and
the pacing, how a story is put together. I've come to measure
my life in pages, stories read and written, and as I get older I
find myself more conscious of time, down to the minute, the
mile and the dollar. My agent continues to believe in me,
continues to set up these meetings, and I take them, always
hoping. "All work," my father used to tell us, "is noble—especially work that pays well." And I wonder if this is why I
find myself in Hollywood again, because I don't make
enough writing novels, if it's just about money, if it's that
simple. I wonder, too, if my brother saw it this way, and if, at
any point in his brief life, he considered it something of a
mistake.

I'm leafing through a copy of *Premiere* when the executive's assistant rises from his desk and walks up to me, this young man

with his hair parted neatly down the middle, and asks if I'd like a cup of coffee, decaf or regular. Or bottled water. Maybe a diet Coke. At this point only twenty minutes have passed since the appointed time.

"It might be a while longer," he says.

He smiles, and by the way he smiles—wry, knowing—he's telling me that I'm in for a wait. Relax, he's saying. The executive is a busy man.

I appreciate his gesture, this small kindness, but I pass on the coffee, decaf or regular, the bottled water and the diet Coke, and after he leaves I wonder how long it'll be before he's moved from the front desk into an office of his own, if he studied literature, art or film in college, or if it was business administration or law. Then I wonder if it matters, if I'm being narrow-minded, defensive for defensiveness's sake, or if I'm just making up excuses to justify my own shortcomings. Good movies are put together by executives as frequently, or as rarely, as they are by anyone else in Hollywood.

Don't prejudge, I tell myself.

Despite my misgivings, despite my ambivalence, I know I'm lucky to get this meeting. Most writers would kill for it.

Around me are other assistants and receptionists, and every now and then, while I wait, one of the office doors opens and someone steps out. An actor maybe. Another writer. And I think—there's my competition. That woman shaking hands with the man in the suit. She's smiling and her eyes look too bright, too excited. Because he probably loved her script. Now she's only a phone call away from her agent who will nail down a deal for a million up front, plus points on the back end, gross not net, and next Sunday I'll spot her picture in the "Calendar" section of the *Los Angeles Times*. Of course I'll be jealous but I certainly won't begrudge her victory. Until today she may have been waiting tables and worrying if she could make this month's rent, and suddenly, after ten years of writing, she's an overnight success.

Something similar happened to a friend of a friend of mine who wrote a movie that later won an Oscar nomination for best screenplay, only it took him closer to fifteen years to become an overnight success. Before that he worked a series of low-paying jobs, and he once confessed to me how it was a terrible strain on his marriage, trying to balance his dream of making it as a writer with the day-to-day realities of making a buck. Back then, just before his big break, he was writing one-liners for the miniature recorders that fit into the plastic cavities of Barbies and Kens.

"It was grueling," he told me. "You rack your fucking brain for a couple hundred lines and then they only take two or three. But they still have to pay you, I mean even for the shit they don't use."

He smiled at me—wry, knowing—just like the executive's assistant had.

"Actually," he said, "it's not bad training for a screenwriter."

I've finished with *Premiere.* I've read *Daily Variety* and the *Hollywood Reporter* cover to cover, including the classifieds. It's five after eleven and my anxiousness has given way to irritation. But I'm not about to voice it. I'm prepared to wait as long as it takes. Two or three hours. The whole day. My main concern is that the executive hasn't forgotten about me, that I'm out here, that I exist in this room with this window overlooking Forest Lawn where my brother is buried. The assistant assures me that it won't be much longer.

"He's wrapping up a deal," he says, "but it's just details now. If he's not done in a few more minutes, I'll drag him out."

Of course I'd like to hear about the deal and its details, even the smallest ones, but I know that it isn't any of my business. So I don't ask. I sit there and wait, and wait, and while I wait I go over my ideas, the ones I turned in to the executive two weeks before. This is the reason for our meeting: to do what's called pitching, and for the executive to suggest which idea, if any, he'd like me to develop further. The same producer who warned me about putting too much ink on the page, all those words, that "black shit," also advised me to keep my ideas short.

One line. Max.

"These guys," he said, "don't like to read."

I have three ideas written in the style of *TV Guide* with its capsulated descriptions, and I've memorized each word for word. The first is a coming-of-age story about a father and son on the run from the law, beginning on the banks of the Willamette River in Oregon and ending in catastrophe in Las Vegas. The second is about a woman who, after fifty years in an abusive marriage, finally leaves her husband and starts a new life for herself at the age of seventy-one. The third idea is about a man who attempts to avenge the murder of his wife and ten-year-old daughter by changing his identity and taking a job as a guard in the maximum-security prison where the killer is incarcerated.

This last sounds the most commercial to me, but it's also the least credible, and the one I'm least inspired to write. I call it *Victims' Rights,* and I know the political and social climate is ripe for a story like it. The second idea isn't thought out yet, although I see potential in the woman's plight, and I believe I could write it with some sense of conviction, of passion. And the first idea, my favorite, is based on the last novel I wrote. Even it sounds crummy to me when reduced to one line, but I like to think that the other lines—all that black shit, over three hundred pages of it—make a difference.

I go over my ideas in my head, word for word, in case the

executive hasn't gotten around to reading them and I have to rattle them off.

"A good pitch shouldn't take more than five minutes," the producer told me. "Max. And cut it short if they start shifting in their seats."

At eleven thirty-five the assistant asks if I'd like to reschedule my appointment. I've been waiting now for over an hour and my lower back aches from sitting too long. The muscles in my neck are tense, and I massage them from time to time, trying to keep them from knotting up. I need to stay calm. I need to relax.

"I'm really sorry about this," he says.

"That's okay," I say. "I'm in no rush."

The assistant rises from his desk.

"I'm going to run and pick up a hamburger before things get too crowded. Want me to get you anything?"

"I'm fine," I say.

He shrugs and then disappears down the hall, the one leading to the elevators. I take a deep breath and tell myself to keep cool. Any second now the executive will step out of his office, smile and call me in. I have to be patient. I have to accept this delay as inevitable, as necessary, as something as basic to the business of moviemaking as gridlock is to the freeways of Los Angeles. It's either that or lose my mind, and as a writer I'm already well on my way. So I take another deep breath. I continue to wait. And while I wait, here on the tenth floor of the Black Tower at Universal Studios, where ideas as ethereal as air are bought and sold for heavenly prices, one of the windows shatters like party ice.

Nobody thinks much of it at first.

Sure, it startles the other assistants and receptionists and myself, too, and the woman closest to this window is actually cut by a shard of glass. Fortunately it isn't a bad cut, hardly a slice along the back of her hand, with no real blood to speak of.

She even shakes her head and laughs.

"Now," she says, "*now* I can collect workers' comp, since mental stress doesn't seem to carry any weight around this god-damn place."

That's when another window blows out. It's on a different floor, but this time we all hear it for what it is, like the back-fire of a distant car, only more hollow sounding. All hell breaks loose after that. Some duck under their desks. Some run for the elevators or race ten flights down the emergency staircase while others crouch behind file cabinets or lock themselves in their offices. I just sit there.

I'm not trying to be brave. Or stupid. I'm as scared as the rest. It's just that I don't know what else to do, what to think or where to run, and despite my mixed feelings about Hollywood I've been waiting a long time for this meeting, if not this particular one on this particular day, then certainly careerwise. Like an earthquake, I expect it to pass soon, and I don't want to appear panicked.

Another window blows out. Again it's on some other floor.

I continue to wait. Two or three minutes pass, and finally the door to the executive's office opens slowly, tentatively, and he peers out at me, a young man with curly red hair. He looks about ten years my junior. I stand up and hold out my hand. He doesn't take it.

"Hello," I say. "I'm Jim Brown."

"Who?"

"Jim Brown. We're supposed to have a meeting today."

"There's a sniper out there," he says. "Are you fucking *crazy*?"

I think about that for a second but decide not to answer. The question that most concerns me is whether or not he's had a chance to look over my ideas and I'm afraid to ask for fear of sounding too anxious, as if it's a matter of life and death.

Ordinarily when I drive into Los Angeles I try to anticipate the unexpected, insofar as that's possible, and compensate for it in advance. Coming, I allow myself that extra time to change a flat tire, say, or if I make the wrong turn and get lost. Going home, if I can't get back on the freeway by two in the afternoon, I'll wait the traffic out until around eight that evening. I'll have a few drinks at a dark quiet bar, maybe some dinner at a fast-food place before I hit the road. But today, both coming and going, my plans backfire.

By the time I leave the Black Tower, the area has already been cordoned off with yellow tape. Studio security and LAPD are everywhere, and as I move through the crowds, on my way to the parking lot, I overhear a man talking.

"It's a tram driver who lost his job," he says. "But they got him already. He was across the street in the park with a high-powered rifle just randomly shooting out windows. Top to bottom. I hope they lock his ass up and throw away the key."

Soon I'm back in my car on the San Bernardino Freeway, heading home. There shouldn't be much traffic now, it's just half-past twelve, but you can't predict when there will be a wreck. Ahead the exhaust from hundreds of cars wavers in the air, liquidlike, and no one is going anywhere. I roll down my window. I light a cigarette and think about the tram driver. He could be a screenwriter. Or better yet an actor. I would bet on it, and his desperation to make it has probably been building for years. Maybe his wife or girlfriend recently left him. Maybe he's drinking too much and can't stop. Each day his disillusionment grows, each day he finds less reason to care. Eventually his frustration turns to anger, the anger to rage, and when he loses his job, a shitty job he never even liked, something inside finally snaps. I can understand that. I can even sympathize.

Slowly the traffic lurches forward. The flashing red and blue lights of the highway patrol come into view, and I see it now—the cause for this delay. It's just a fender bender but still everyone has to stop and stare. We're all looking for blood. We're all expecting the worst. Mangled frames of cars. Shattered glass. Anything short of someone being carried away on a stretcher is a disappointment.

MY PAPA'S WALTZ

We have an old reel-to-reel tape recorder, and when my father gets drunk he puts on Patsy Cline's song "Crazy" and asks me to dance. He has this sloppy smile on his face. I'm six, maybe seven years old at the time. He is in his midfifties and his drunken sentimentality annoys me. His palms feel rough and hard when he slips them into mine and tries to lift me from my chair at the kitchen table. But I hold tight to the edge, the chipped green Formica, or one of the slick chrome legs. "Up, up," he says. "Let go. Dance." His breath smells of whiskey, his collar of sawdust and sweat. My father is a building contractor, a good one, a real finish man who charges people according to what he thinks they can afford, and they often take advantage of him.

A few years back I wrote a novel that uses this memory as its heart. I've mined the territory before, if not this particular moment then something like it, and I've done it so often that I find myself confusing what actually happened with how I imagine it. In trying to sort between autobiography and fiction, or invention, and then trying to put the pieces together so that they make some kind of sense, I've come to think that the truth as it occurs isn't of much use to me other than, say, as a catalyst for a story. While I'm figuring this out, I lose a couple of years writing a bad novel. I don't get through it and that's a good thing, because if I hadn't given up I would have lost more time. And I worry about time.

The problem, at least one of them, was that I was being dishonest with myself in the worst, most shameful way. I was writing about people and events and places that I didn't fully understand, and I wasn't good enough at it for it not to show. So I start another book, one that makes me see past what I think actually occurred, to what hasn't but *should have* according to that thing I imagine called plot. And the writer's obsession, as I also come to understand, suggests something other than limitation or theme, that as storytellers we basically spend our lives telling the same story over and over, only we do it from different angles.

The trick is disguising it, so it doesn't seem the same.

The trick is how well you can keep doing it, not once or

twice, but hundreds of times, page after page, with one real detail after another. The hardest part is to make it appear seamless and vivid in the end as if it all came naturally.

Like magic.

Like you don't have to think. Like it really couldn't have happened any other way.

I was in college when I encountered "My Papa's Waltz," Theodore Roethke's short dark poem about dancing with his drunken father. I don't know for a fact if Roethke ever danced with his father and I don't believe that it matters. Of course, when I'm six or seven years old, I'd never heard of the poet, and it wouldn't have made any difference if I had. Reading is for sissies, especially poems, and like my old man I consider myself a tough guy. Pound for pound I can kick any kid's ass in the neighborhood, and where we live on the poor side of San Jose I have some serious competition. My mother is in prison at the time, and my father, my brother and sister and I share a one-bedroom apartment with a kitchenette and a hot plate, a window overlooking the warehouse next door and a sofa bed in the living room. You have to push it back into place in the morning, so you can get to the bathroom.

William Street Park is only a few blocks away, and I spend plenty of hot summer days playing around the creek that passes through it. It was a rough place then and it's no better now, with all the dope and every other kid carrying a piece. The generation has changed. The clothes are different. But the pose is the same. Black kids still hang out on the benches and behind the bathrooms, glossy eyed, getting wasted, and the *pachucos* or *cholos,* what they call *homies* now, are on the other side of the park at the mouth of the old drain storm tunnel that runs under the street. My father buys the old reel-to-reel recorder here, off some older guy who needs a few quick bucks.

I like the tunnel. On the hottest days, when everybody is dragging, I stop about halfway through the tunnel and suck the cool air deep into my lungs. I like to press my cheek against the cool steel and feel the vibrations of the cars and the trucks rumbling past on the street above. I think about my mother. I think about when she's coming home. My old man doesn't like to talk about it and I'm left to wonder, to make up stories. To imagine. I plan the Great Escape in that tunnel and play it over and over in my head.

I need rope.

I need a gun.

I need a guard's uniform and a pair of walkie-talkies, so that my father and I can coordinate our actions, working from the inside and out. The first two items are easily had; the rope I buy, a hundred feet of good nylon five-hundred-pound test, and my father owns a German Luger. We'll steal her away to

Mexico in our Chevy stepside. But there's a catch. Finding a guard's uniform to fit a sixty-pound kid will take some doing.

It isn't funny, either.

Every detail has to work or I will fail.

Lives, real or imagined, are at stake.

In that novel I wrote, a father plays a prominent role in a boy's life. His mother disappears years before. The boy, the narrator, can't recall knowing her, because she deserts him before he has the power of memory, and toward the end of the book he decides to pull up stakes and go looking for her. In my own life, when I try to remember exactly what happens the night that my father asks me to dance, I get confused.

Maybe it isn't 1962 in that cramped apartment on the poor side of San Jose. Maybe it's 1963. Maybe I'm closer to eight than seven, and why my mother is sent to prison doesn't really matter because she is never coming back, not the same woman anyway, and what I did know of her—*before*—is little more than imagined.

For dancing, I am too awkward, too timid and full of anger and blindness. But when I write today, when I write now, when I write *this*, the drunken smile on my father's face no longer annoys me. I let him take my hands and guide me across the cracked and yellowed linoleum floor in that kitchenette with Patsy Cline playing on the old reel-to-reel tape recorder that is probably stolen. I feel the warm harsh breath of his whisper in my ear and I smell the whiskey. I smell the sawdust and sweat.

"Smile," he says. "Dance. Your momma's coming home to-morrow."

That's fiction. But, in fact, it doesn't matter.

I let go of the table and dance with my father and the song is always "Crazy."

THE FACTS

Someone is watching me. Someone has been watching me off and on now for sixteen hours. But every time I look out the window he slips behind the refrigerator in the yard of the abandoned house down the street. All I see is his pants leg. All I see is one foot, a tennis shoe, before he ducks out of view. This is happening to me at the E-Z Eight Motel on Macarthur Boulevard in Oakland. I haven't slept or eaten in three days. I check the locks on the door again. I check the window and turn away. On the TV a young woman is fucking two men and I watch them for a while. It's four o'clock in the morning, and in a few hours I have to lecture on *Huckleberry Finn* to a class of undergraduates.

In the bathroom mirror I look at myself. My eyes are bloodshot. My face is drawn and pasty and there's a distinct chemical odor emanating from the pores of my skin. Over the last few weeks my weight has dropped from a hundred and seventy pounds to a hundred and forty, and I've lost the feeling in two fingers on my left hand. Nerve damage. A short circuit in the brain. I look closer. There are delicate, threadlike patterns of broken blood vessels along the bridge of my nose. The condition is called spider angioma, and it comes from drinking heavily over a long period of time, when the liver can no longer freely cleanse the blood and it begins to clot. The tiny vessels burst. I know this because my brother had it. I know this because I've read dozens of books on alcoholism and drug addiction, though none of them, no amount of knowledge, has helped me to stop.

I undress. I turn on the hot water, only the hot water, and step into the shower and bear it for as long as I can. The pain distracts. The pain is good, and when I step out I am pink all over, the flesh tender and inflamed. Naked, I return to the bed and lie down, my arms to my sides, like a corpse. The movie is still playing, a continuous loop, but now the scene offers two women. They're stretched out on a bed in what looks like a motel room, a motel room like this, with a loud bedspread and cheap vinyl furniture. One is only wearing a garter belt and stockings. The other is dressed in tight jeans and a halter top.

I want to keep watching them but instead I shut my eyes. Sleep is what I need, even if it's only for a few minutes, but my body is a live wire. I get up and go to the window again and peer through a break in the drapes. The streets are empty and quiet and most of the apartments and houses that line the block have bars on their windows and doors. The sun is just rising and so far as I can tell I'm no longer being watched. That or he's hiding somewhere else. At best this is only a temporary reprieve and yet I'm thankful for it. I am relieved.

At the corner an older Buick pulls to the curb and a woman steps out. She crosses the street, a little unsteadily in her heels, and when she disappears I turn away from the window and start to dress. I put on a pair of wrinkled Levi's and the oxford shirt that I wore to class last Friday. I comb my hair. I use my finger to brush my teeth. Then I put Visine in my eyes and stand before the mirror and try to convince myself that I look like something other than a drug addict. By the time I leave the motel the morning traffic has begun and soon I'm surrounded by other cars and trucks on Interstate 580, all of us moving at a steady seventy miles an hour, all of us trailing closely together.

If the car ahead suddenly threw on its brakes, I wouldn't be able to stop in time. Neither would the car tailgating me. In an instant the freeway would be littered with bodies, steel and glass. I hold the wheel tightly and concentrate on the road.

Ahead my exit is approaching, and I need to change lanes. There's an opening but I don't trust myself, whether I looked carefully enough, so I check again. I check three, four times. A mistake at this speed in rush-hour traffic is deadly, and I know I shouldn't be here, that I have no right to be behind the wheel of a car. But I make it, as I have so many times before, in even worse condition, and once I'm safely parked in the school lot I take a deep breath, thankful to have again reached my destination alive. I light a cigarette and just sit there for a while, smoking, listening to the engine tick itself cool. On the radio the weatherman predicts another bright sunny day.

The month is October but for the last several weeks temperatures have been in the eighties. Students are dressed as if it were still summer, the young women in shorts and skirts, the young men in T-shirts and rubber sandals, and as I start across campus I wish for dark skies. I wish for black clouds and strong winds and rain, hard rain, the kind that washes out roads. The kind that knocks down power lines. But the sky is perfectly clear. Already I've begun to sweat.

My briefcase is heavy with papers and books—*The Norton Anthology of Literature, The Story and Its Writer,* the Bantam edition of *Huckleberry Finn*—and two classes' worth of undergraduate essays, about sixty in all, that I can't bring myself to read. The students will be disappointed. I said I would have them back today. I said I would have them back the week before and now

I have to offer up another excuse, another promise I may fully intend to keep but which I will most likely break. My office is on the third floor of the humanities building, and though I'm short of breath I take the stairs. I take them because I don't want to risk being trapped in the elevator with someone who knows me and having to carry on the pretense of a polite conversation. I'm not ready for that yet, or the crowds, all the people. All the noise and commotion. I need to ease into this slowly, retreat to my office, lock the door and do another line.

The hallway is long and narrow and the walls on both sides seem to merge at the end, into a point, like a diagram in perspective. The fluorescent lights overhead seem extraordinarily bright. Some of the professors are in their offices, and to get to mine I have to pass by their open doors.

The trick, I tell myself, is to stare at the floor. To walk quickly.

I almost make it.

The professor in the office directly across from mine is at her desk having a conference with a young Japanese student. She speaks slowly and loudly as if she's instructing the deaf. Teaching English as a second language is her specialty and she addresses all of her foreign students in this manner. While I'm fumbling with my keys, trying to get the right one into the lock, she glances over at me.

"You look like hell," she says.

"What?"

"I said you look like hell."

"I've been up all weekend," I say. "Working on my book."

"Yeah," she says, "right."

I resent her snide remarks, I resent her as a person for talking down to her students, but I'm in no condition to react. All I want is to escape into my office. She says something else—something rude, I imagine—which I don't catch because I've finally gotten the door open, stepped inside and shut it behind me. I lock it. I check it just to be sure and then I take the small plastic bag from my pocket and empty it onto my desk. I have a razor in my wallet and I use it to cut the crystals into a fine white powder and draw them into two long lines. The rest I return to the bag. For a straw, I roll up a dollar bill. The tissues inside my nose are swollen and raw, I've been bleeding, and it's several tries before I can do the first line. It makes my eyes water, it burns, and I like it. In a matter of seconds all the fear and paranoia, all the things I don't want to think about or feel, slip away. I take a deep breath again. I let it out slowly and wish that I were someplace, anywhere but here. The next line is easier.

My wife hasn't heard from me since I left Friday night. What we fought about, I don't remember, but I imagine that it had to do with money. It always seems to be about money at first and then turns into something else. I pick up the phone.

I make the call. It rings and rings, and as it continues to ring it crosses my mind that this could be the last time, this could be the end. I picture an empty house. I picture empty closets and unmade beds. But then she answers, slightly out of breath.

In the background I can hear our second child, Logan, crying loud and sharply. He is three years old and so far he has not been as easy to raise as his brother. His eyes are highly sensitive to light, his ears to noise, and he cries often, constantly testing his mother's patience. Usually I'm the one to calm him, to hold and walk the boy until his chest stops heaving. He is more used to my arms than hers.

"Honey," I say, "it's me."

"What do you want?"

"We need to talk."

"I hate you," she says, and hangs up.

I call back. She answers on the first ring this time but doesn't say anything. I tell her I'm sorry. That I want to come home. I go on like this for a couple of minutes before she cuts me off.

"Just do what the fuck you want," she says. "You always do anyway."

Then she hangs up.

From my office window I can see San Francisco Bay, the waters a greenish-blue. Beyond it is the coastline, and if I left now I could be there in an hour, cruising along Highway 1. I want to get in the car and drive and drive but I know I won't. I know I can't. Classes have begun, and already I'm a few minutes late. I grab my briefcase and hurry out of the office.

I dim the lights when I come into the room. I draw the blinds and try to keep my hands from shaking. The students are quiet. At the podium I fumble for my notes. I almost drop the book. Someone laughs, and I look up. It's a kid in the back, a freshman with purple hair and a spiked dog collar around his neck. "Another rough weekend, Professor Brown?" he says. The girl sitting next to him laughs. The rest don't see the humor in it, and I appreciate them for it. They're a range of ages and colors but mostly they're older. Housewives returning to school after raising their families. Middle-aged men frustrated with their careers and trying to start a new one. I have a guy in his seventies who comes to class with an oxygen tank. I am in my early thirties. The course is a standard comp and lit, required of all English and liberal arts majors.

On the board I write the words *guilt, compassion, humility.* Beneath that I write *Jim as moral instructor* and then I begin to read aloud from chapter 22. It's about a lynch mob who set out after a man named Sherburn because he killed the town drunk for disgracing him in public. And considering my condition I think I'm doing an excellent job of it. My mouth is dry but I read clearly. I go at just the right pace. I pause in all the right places. When I first walked into class and looked out over all those faces I wasn't sure if I'd make it, if I ought to just dismiss them and save myself the embarrassment. But my confidence grows as I continue to read. I'm on the scene now where Sherburn confronts the mob for the cowards they are; it's one of my favorite parts, and as I pace in front of the class reading with more passion, it suddenly occurs to me that my notes on the board have absolutely nothing to do with the material at hand. The scene I intended to talk about isn't even in this chapter. That's when I lose my rhythm and begin to stutter.

An older student raises her hand.

"Excuse me," she says. "But I think you went over this last week."

No one laughs this time, though I wish they had. The silence has less to do with respect than compassion for something pathetic. Ordinarily it wouldn't be such a big deal—professors get mixed up all the time—but because I'm hungover and strung out and have no business being here, I feel I have to justify myself. I try to look surprised at my mistake. I make an act of checking our syllabus, and finally I smile, admit the error and shake my head.

A young woman in the front row catches my eye. Her name is Sylvia Garcia. She's a shy, unassuming student who sometimes brings her little boy to class with her, and when I'm conscious of being a good teacher I make a point of calling on the quieter ones. I want to involve everyone. In Sylvia's case, however, that proves a mistake. The word *nigger* appears three times in the passage I ask her to read, and though I encourage my students to refer to Jim as Jim, as I do, even when the text uses *nigger*, I don't require it. The only rule is to remain true to the spirit of the story. That's why I don't initially interrupt her. The first time could be a mistake, the stress she puts on it. The second time is clearly not. There's a slight but certain venom in her voice. It's as if she enjoys saying *nigger*, as if she's been given a license to offend because it's there in print.

"Sylvia," I say, "there's no reason for that."

"What're you talking about?"

"You know exactly what I mean."

She gives me a wide-eyed, innocent look.

"No," she says, "I don't. Tell me."

Now I wonder if maybe I'm wrong, if maybe I'm imagining things, or being overly sensitive. I don't think so. Another student, a black woman, gets up and leaves the room.

For a while the class is dead quiet. Everyone is staring at me, and I don't know what to do, whether to turn today's lesson into a discussion on race or pretend that nothing has happened and continue where we left off. Either way I'm bound to fail. I take the path of least resistance and dismiss them early. No one protests. No one even seems to care.

The rest of the day is uneventful, and I'm grateful for it, though I regret having wasted the class and the students' time.

They deserve much better. I return to my office, lock the door and spend the next few hours trying to get through a stack of short stories from my next class, Creative Writing 101. The first is set on a spaceship that's under attack by alien creatures. Another all takes place in the mind of a teenage girl but we don't know where she's at until the last line when it's revealed that she's about to have an abortion. I've read them before, if not these particular stories then something very much like them. I've read them so often that I don't know what to say about them anymore that doesn't sound cynical or mean-spirited. Sometimes I think about turning them back with a match taped to the last page. Instead I write things in the margins like *great image* or *well done* or *good job* or *Yes,* with an exclamation point, and at the end of the story I comment briefly in still more general terms. I've only been at this university for a year, as a writer-in-residence, my first real job out of graduate school, and because of the alcohol and drugs I already feel burned-out.

It rarely happens but the student whose work is due for review today turns up absent. I keep the class waiting for twenty minutes and then, like the first, I let them leave early. Normally I teach three courses each term but the dean of the School of Humanities and the chair of the English department have rewarded me with one less class for recently winning a literary award and publishing a novel called *Final Performance.* So I'm through for the day except for keeping my office hours, which I have no intention of doing. By now it's maybe two, three in the afternoon and I need a drink to steady my nerves. I need a drink before I can face my wife and kids.

On the drive home I stop at a liquor store and buy a half pint of Smirnoff. That's all I want. I've resolved, on a whim, that I should at least try to limit myself today. But of course it doesn't work that way. I live in the town of Santa Clara, about forty miles from the university, and by the time I pull off the freeway the bottle is empty and I need another. Trouble is, I made a resolution to limit myself and I'm determined to stick to it. It's supposed to be about choice, about willpower, but once the craving kicks in I don't seem to have much of either. So instead of buying another bottle I make a pact with myself, and as a compromise, because there's always room for compromise, I agree to one last drink. That's all. No more. And as further proof of my commitment that last drink has to be beer. There are three dingy little bars on the way to my house, when I pull off the freeway, and I choose the closest one. Before I go in I check my watch. It's just after four. A couple of old Harleys are parked out front, the chrome shining in the sun.

The jukebox only plays old rock and roll but no one is putting in any quarters. Except for a listless barmaid staring at a silent TV, and a couple of gray-haired bikers drinking in the corner, the place is dead. It's dark and quiet and I like it this way. There are no potted ferns hanging from the ceiling. There are no bright, airy windows and they don't make strawberry daiquiris or fluorescent-green margaritas. You come here to drink and the drinks are cheap. I get my beer and then go to the pay phone outside the bathrooms and call my wife to let her know I'm on my way.

We have two children at this point in time, our third and last son has yet to be born, and the older one answers. He's only seven but he's smart and grown-up for his years, maybe too smart and grown-up. Over and over he's seen his father loaded and strung out and I know it scares him. I know it hurts him as it hurts his mother, and time and again he has had to come to her aid. To comfort her. No child should have to live under these circumstances, and I worry that one day he will grow up to be just like his old man. For all this I feel deep shame, and yet, without explanation, it isn't enough to keep me from drinking and drugging.

"Hey, Andy," I say.

"Dad?"

He says it like he's surprised to hear from me. That I'm alive.

"Where've you been?" he asks. "Are you okay?"

"I'm fine. Put your mom on."

He calls out to her from across the living room. A few seconds pass. I take a drink from my beer. Then he gets back on the line and says, "She doesn't want to talk to you."

"Tell her it's important."

"Mom," he calls out, "he says it's important."

I can't quite make out what she says but her tone is clear enough.

"Did you hear that?" Andy says.

"No," I say.

"Good," he says.

"Just tell her I'll be home for dinner."

I say good-bye and hang up and return to my bar stool. My beer is almost gone, and because I still have a couple of hours to kill before dinner, and because beer is so low in alcohol you can't honestly count having just one as a bona fide drink, I order another. In the back of my mind I know that I'm rationalizing but at this particular moment, sitting in a dark and quiet bar, it all makes perfect sense. The next time I look at my watch it's after midnight.

The house we rent is on a tree-lined street in a middle-class neighborhood in Santa Clara. It's pitch-black out and so quiet that I can hear my ears ringing. I know my wife hears me pull into the driveway. I know my car wakes her. But I also know that she won't be out of bed to confront me tonight. That will come later, tomorrow morning, after she returns from dropping our older son off at school. Quietly I let myself into the house and fumble through the dark, down the staircase leading to the basement that I've made into an office. I turn on the desk lamp. I take a sleeping bag from the storage closet and spread it open on the floor.

As a nightcap I do another line. It's the last of my dope and the thought of running out panics me but there's nothing I can do about it, at least not now. I undress and turn out the light and get into the sleeping bag. My heart is pumping hard. I imagine it bursting, the fluids draining, seeping out, filling me up. I close my eyes and clips from the movie at the motel flash through my mind. A woman and two men. Two women together. Then suddenly I hear a rustling noise outside, the snapping of twigs. At first I think it might be the raccoons that live in the sewer and come out at night to hunt for food. I listen more intently, and when I hear it again I climb slowly to my feet and peer through the basement window that looks out over the driveway. A tall maple grows at the curb, and I see something duck behind it. The outline of a shoulder. The shape of a head.

He's there and then he's not.

I don't know if I'm hallucinating. Or just paranoid. But I continue to stare. Paranoia, I tell myself, is a man with the facts.

And the facts, for this man, are these: I am no kind of father. I am no kind of husband. No kind of teacher. I am instead that man I see and don't see and he is watching me, as I am watching him, both of us afraid to step out from the darkness.

TOUCH

A man in my apartment complex wants to take pictures of me. He says I am naturally photogenic. He says that one of the boys he photographed recently signed a modeling contract with the Broadway stores. "Have you ever thought about modeling or acting?" He leans against the hand railing. His dress shirt is rumpled in front and stained under the arms. I look down at the pool in the courtyard below. The water is soft blue and white. Threads of light reflect beneath the surface, and in the evening I like to come out here and watch them, how they twist and bend, these threads of light. I am twelve years old.

"My brother's the actor," I say.

"What's he done?"

"A movie of the week." I say this casually, as my brother does, as if it's not a big deal. But it is a big deal and I'm proud of him. "It airs in September." The word *airs,* I think, makes me sound more mature. It's also the word Barry uses.

It is humid and I am alone in the hallway when the man comes up the stairs that night we first met. I've seen him around before, many times, but until now we have never spoken. He carries a long black equipment case and the weight of it pulls at his arm, making one look longer than the other. The apartment door is open and he stops and glances inside. The TV is on but there's nothing worth watching. This is the beginning of the summer rerun season. "I know we're neighbors," he says, "but I've never stopped to say hello." He puts down his equipment case and holds out his hand to shake. His palm is cool, his grip loose. Ranchero music rises from one of the apartments below. "I'm Earl, from apartment 22," he says. In the dim light of the hallway I feel him staring.

Before he leaves he gives me his business card. I appreciate the gesture, that he treats me as an adult, but I have no use for it. He is just another person in the building I don't care to know. I rest my elbows on the railing, turning the card over in my hands. There is no rush to go back inside. My mother is working late and won't be home until after ten. My sister is supposed to be staying the night at a friend's house but she's really at the beach with her boyfriend. I overheard her plans on the phone and promised not to tell. And our brother, he has his own place now, a one-room studio in Hollywood a couple miles from here. I went by earlier hoping to surprise him but he wasn't there.

Down the hall, the kitchen light comes on in Earl's apartment. Then it goes out and he draws the drapes over the living room window, lit up now by the blue-gray flicker of his TV. I fold the card in half and tear it along the crease. I do this several times and then let the pieces fall, like confetti, into the threads of light that move along the bottom of the pool.

On the surface it's about money, but it's really about control. She is happy for him. She is proud that he landed his first serious role in a movie of the week. But she has also invested years of her life in helping him build his career and expects more of the paycheck than he's willing to share. Barry has graduated from high school with a 4.0, he's already been dreaming of moving out for quite a while, and these recent troubles with our mother just give him all the more reason to go. He is no fool. If he stays, he knows that nothing will ever change. I know it, too, and I encourage him to leave. But it's been two months now and I miss him. That he lives nearby is no consolation if he's rarely at home.

In those first few weeks after he leaves he makes a point of finding time for me. Twice he lets Marilyn and me sleep over and we stay up until the early morning hours listening to music and drinking beer and talking. He gives Marilyn the bed. He and I sleep on the floor, and when we wake up he takes us to the House of Pancakes on Sunset Boulevard for a late breakfast. But things soon change. Once he has that first credit, his agent sends him out more regularly, and he's getting attention, he's generating interest.

"I'm up for three shows," he tells us over breakfast. "Two are callbacks. I'm close. Real close," he says. "Maybe then I can help you guys more." He drinks from his coffee. "But you know I couldn't stay there. I mean with Mom."

I don't know if in those earlier weeks he'd been trying to wean us from him, or if, as the days continue to pass, he just finds himself too busy. Either way, missing him doesn't get easier with time. Where before he always returned my phone calls quickly, now it takes him two or three days, sometimes longer, and I begin to think that he doesn't care anymore. That I'm a pest. That he's outgrown my company. Inside I believe differently, but then I have also learned not to trust myself. What I'm trying to say here is that at this point in time I am very young and vulnerable. And when you are very young and vulnerable you may make a mistake. You may be scared. You may be reckless. Most likely, you don't think at all.

I'm standing in the magic shop on Hollywood Boulevard, looking at the masks lined neatly along the shelves behind the counter. There is Bela Lugosi as Count Dracula. There is Lon Chaney as the Werewolf. There is Frankenstein and the Creature from the Black Lagoon but my favorite is the one of Tor Johnson with the jagged scar that runs from the top of his round bald head to the corner of his left eye. He is scowling. I am trying to remember the name of the movie, the one with the scene where he stares up at you from inside a sewer, through the black iron grate, when I see Earl at the counter. It's a coincidence but not a stretch. His studio is on Cahuenga, a block off the boulevard, and it's his lunch hour. He is walking by and spots me in the window.

The clerk approaches.

"Can I help you, sir?"

"Let me see that one," he says, pointing. "The one the boy's looking at."

It's made of rubber, the kind of mask that covers the whole head, and he has to work it on slowly. The rubber pulls at his hair, pinches the flesh around his chubby ears. With it on he turns to me and holds both arms out as if he's just risen from the grave. He makes a low, growling noise.

"That's pretty lame," I say.

He laughs and pulls off the mask. In that short time he's already begun to sweat.

"Don't lie. I can tell you're scared." He turns to the clerk. "How much?" he says.

"Forty bucks."

"I don't want it," I say.

Earl looks over his shoulder at me. "Who said it was for you?"

Pink's Famous Hot Dog stand is across the street on the corner, and I follow him there from the magic shop, out of politeness, too shy to turn down his invitation. We sit on red vinyl stools at the counter and eat greasy chili dogs, not talking, not a word. It's another hot smoggy day. The sidewalks are crowded with summer tourists, and as I watch them pass I wonder how it is that anyone could find Hollywood glamorous. Next door is a tattoo parlor. Farther down it's the Pussycat Theater and a leather bar. Every block has the same old T-shirt shops, and at the end of the day, when the different businesses turn out the lights, what you can't find in the stores is sold openly from their alcoves at night. My brother has bought grass here half a dozen times.

From under the counter Earl slips the bag from the magic shop into my lap.

"Thanks," I tell him, "but I can't take it."

"Can't or won't?"

I set the bag on the counter beside him and he opens it. Holds out the mask.

"Try it on."

"Here?"

"Yeah, here. What do you care what people think?"

I hesitate.

"Go on," he says. "Don't be a pussy."

The mask slips easily over my head. I like the strong smell of the rubber but it's hard to breathe and the eyes of the mask don't line up with my own. That's when it comes to me. *The Unearthly.* The name of the movie I couldn't remember. Or maybe, on second thought, it's *Mr. Sardonicus.* My brother took me to both. "Hey," someone says, "a monster." From somewhere along the counter I hear laughter.

I pull off the mask and hand it to him. But he won't take it, he waves it away. "It fits you perfectly. Keep it." He sips from his Coke. He smiles. "Sometimes," he says, "you have to go along with people, even if you don't want to, because it makes them happy."

At twelve I'm not very good at guessing an adult's age. But I am forty-three years old as I write this, and when I look back, when I remember that smile and how his stare lingered, I see the face of a plain, average-looking young man. His hair had already begun to thin and gray on the sides but he couldn't have been any more than twenty-four, twenty-five. His skin is what makes me think this. It is smooth in my memory, unblemished from the passing of too many years, and his hands as I remember them, and I remember them well, are as soft as those of any woman who's ever touched me.

✳   ✳   ✳

In the middle of the kitchen table is a lazy Susan that our mother and father brought back from their trip to Honolulu before the breakup. It is a relic of the past, somehow surviving our family upheavals through the years, our many moves where too many things get lost or broken or simply left behind. Perched at the top of the center post is the hand carving of a little girl wearing a grass skirt and a lei. She is captured in the pose of dance, her arms swaying to one side, the hips cocked in a rolling motion. In the wooden dishes surrounding her are smoked oysters, cashews, baby corns, green olives stuffed with pimentos, potato chips and garlic dip. I look closely at the carving, the stiff smile cut into her lips. Then I stab a toothpick into the open half of a deviled egg and push it into my mouth.

"That's it, no more," my mother says.

"I'm starving," I say.

"Too bad. You just have to wait."

On the kitchen counter is a bottle of Korbel, and she pours the last of it into her champagne glass, the rim stained red from her lipstick. She is wearing a bright yellow apron and fuzzy white slippers and the half-moons of exhaustion weigh heavy beneath her eyes. Our father sends her little money, he is struggling himself back in San Jose, and so our mother must work long hours, weeks on end without a day off until now. Tonight is about making up for lost time, all the fast food we've eaten, TV dinners and frozen chicken pot pies. Tonight is about declaring a truce with her older son, her favorite son, who is supposed to have been here a half hour ago. It will be our first dinner together since he moved out.

A pot of spicy marinara sauce simmers on the stove. She stirs it with a wooden spoon and calls out. "Marilyn . . . Marilyn." The door to Marilyn's room opens and she peers out from around the side. Her hair is wrapped in a towel, and you can hear the music behind her, louder now with the door open. Rock and roll. The Beatles' *White Album.*

"What'd you want?"

"Tell your boyfriend good-bye. You have to get off the phone."

"In a minute."

"Now," she says. "Your brother might be trying to call."

Marilyn slams the door, so hard the kitchen window rattles. A moment later the music grows louder, and our mother takes off her apron, tosses it on the couch. I think at first that she's going after her, that she intends to set her straight, but instead she heads toward the bathroom. "I better get ready," she tells me. "Would you mind opening another bottle of champagne? Just hold it over the sink, so you don't make a mess."

I have made her drinks before, two shots of Old Crow and a splash of Coke, vodka and V-8, or just neat with a pickled onion if it's been a particularly long day. But champagne is her favorite, reserved only for special occasions, and I've never opened a bottle of it. Because Barry is older and stronger this would ordinarily be his job, and though I've watched him do it many times before I am still nervous as I peel back the label, untwist the wire and take hold of the plastic cork. I work it back and forth and soon it rises, on its own accord, pushing against my hand. I push back but the pressure is suddenly too great. The cork flies across the kitchen, bounces off the wall, and I hold my mouth over the stream of champagne so it won't spill onto the floor. I swallow quickly, several mouthfuls, and when the stream subsides I tilt the bottle back and swallow some more.

When my mother returns she is wearing a black dress, a color she thinks makes her look thinner. She has always had a problem with her weight, ballooning up for months at a time and then starving herself, subsisting on celery, radishes and water. It's a cycle. It's a constant struggle, and since Barry left she has put on more weight than ever. Most of it goes to her thighs. The black dress fits too tightly, and her nylons make a faint scratching noise as she passes through the living room, back to the kitchen. The clock on the wall shows that it's quarter after eight. He is over an hour late, yet she continues to prepare, ignoring the obvious. She sets the table with care, laying out her best place mats and matching cloth napkins, adjusting them just so, humming to herself. I want to tell her that she is wasting her time but I don't. I know better. Instead I say, "C'mon, sit down for a while. Let me pour you another glass of champagne." By now I am feeling the effects of it myself and no longer have an appetite.

Later that night, after she's passed out on the couch, my sister slips out of her room. "I'll be right back," she says. "I have to get some hairspray." She locks the door on her way out, and I get up. I phone my brother. But all I reach is his answering service, a harried woman on the other end of the line. "Tell him his brother called," I say. "Tell him he was supposed to come by for dinner." I hang up and return to the living room and sit back down on the floor beside the couch. The TV is on but the sound is turned low. It's the only light in the room, and for a while I just watch the rise and fall of her chest, her gentle breathing. On her finger is the wedding band and diamond that my father gave her, and I remember asking about it, why after all these years she still wears it. She tells me it's to ward off other men, that another man is the very last thing she needs in this life. Somehow I don't believe her. I take her hand in mine, the same hand that holds a steak knife to my brother's throat when he tells her that he is leaving. But I prefer to think of other times. I prefer to rest my head on the cushion beside her and feel the warmth through the coarse fabric of her black dress.

✳   ✳   ✳

It is worse at night. It is worse when the apartment is quiet and I'm lying in bed across from where my brother used to sleep. Now his bed is stripped to the mattress. Now his dresser is gone as well as the bookcases and all the books that I helped him pack into boxes and label with a black felt pen. Fiction. Film. History. On the wall, where glossies of Montgomery Clift and James Dean once hung, there is only the vague outline of the frames, the brighter spots of paint. These nights, they just pass, one into another, and I have this sickening feeling inside that I am losing something more than a brother.

I have few friends, no close ones, anyway, of the sort that make a difference, and I spend most of my mornings stretched out on the couch watching TV. I don't get dressed before noon. Later, maybe, I take myself to a movie or blow off a few hours dropping quarters into the pinball machines in the arcades on Hollywood Boulevard. By then it's growing dark, and instead of going back to an empty apartment I hang out at Plummer Park for a while. Usually the baseball field is lit with stadium lights. Usually there's a softball game, adult teams, and I sit at the top of the bleachers and watch them for a while, rooting with the crowd, cheering the hits, pretending I belong.

His guitar strap reminds me of the blankets I've seen hanging in the open markets in Tijuana. It's made of the same material, the same pattern and garish colors, and that's what first catches my eye. Though it's still light out, the living room is dark. The shades are drawn, and as I reach for the light switch I see movement, I glimpse the strap. They're on the couch, my sister and José, the boyfriend who carries his guitar wherever he goes and sings Spanish love songs to her. He has her blouse open and is working his hand into her pants. I don't know who's more shocked, me or them, but they both jump back, knocking the guitar off the couch.

"You're in deep shit," I say. "Just wait till Mom gets home."

She holds her blouse together with one fist and flies up at me with the other.

"C'mere, you little creep."

I've felt her blows before, and she isn't even close when I'm back out the door. She stops at the threshold and hollers down the hall.

"I'm serious," she says. "You better keep your trap shut."

It's late in the afternoon and the rush-hour traffic has begun. I walk quickly, keeping my head down, concentrating on my steps. My brother lives in an older building in the heart of Hollywood, a tall, ten-story building that looks as if it were once a lavish hotel. In its glory days it was probably a nice place to live but now the paint is peeling off the stucco walls and most of the window screens are torn or missing. The ivy along the walkway is yellowed and dying, and inside the lobby, where a clerk works behind a sheet of bulletproof glass, it smells of mold and the powerful cleansers used to mask it. I step into the elevator. It creaks and groans as it rises, taking me to the sixth floor. From there I walk down the hall to my brother's room and knock on the door. Music plays softly from inside. I knock again, louder. He answers this time, wearing only a towel wrapped around his waist. His hair is wet and freshly combed and one side of his face is covered with shaving cream. My brother is handsome, dark-complexioned from the Sicilian on our mother's side. People tell me we look alike, and though I'd like to believe them, I don't see much of my brother in myself.

"What're you doing here?"

I shrug.

"I just thought I'd drop by."

"You should've called first. I have to leave in a few minutes. But come on in," he says, "we'll talk while I'm getting ready."

He returns to the bathroom but leaves the door open. I wander around the room. There's a bed and nightstand in one corner and a service kitchen in the other with a small refrigerator and a hot plate. His books are carefully arranged on their shelves, even the paperbacks. The one window overlooks the rooftops of the stores and shops along Hollywood Boulevard, and in the distance, if you lean out and look east you can see the Capitol Records Tower on Vine Street. On the nightstand is an ashtray, and in it are several cigarette butts, the filters stained red. I pick one up.

"What's she look like?" I say.

"Who?"

"Your girlfriend."

"I don't have a girlfriend."

I hold up the cigarette butt.

"What's this?" I say. "She the reason you missed dinner last week?"

He pokes his head out from around the bathroom door. "That," he says, smiling, "is none of your goddamn business."

I go to the refrigerator and open it. All he has are a few cans of Budweiser and an old package of Oscar Mayer bologna and a near empty jar of mayonnaise. I help myself to a beer and then lean against the doorjamb of the bathroom and watch him shave. He looks at me in the mirror, and for a second I think he's about to reprimand me for drinking. Instead he tilts his head back and draws the razor slowly under his chin.

"That better not be my last," he says.

"You got two more."

"Good," he says. "Why don't you get me one."

And I think to myself, Yes, this is what it's like. To be on your own. To be a man. No one telling you what you can or can't do.

"You mind if I stay over?" I say.

"Not tonight."

"How come?"

He gives me that smile again.

"I might have company later. Hey," he says, "where's my beer?"

In the window of the studio are high school graduation portraits. The young men wear tuxedos. The young women wear formals cut low in the front. They are all carefully posed, chins raised, staring off into the distance as if looking toward their future. Hanging above them are wedding portraits in big gold baroque frames, the couples looking dreamily into each other's eyes. There are also pictures of babies and children and another of a Welsh terrier with a pink ribbon tied in a bow on the top of its head. Even though the sign on the door reads CLOSED, I see Earl inside behind the counter, still working. I tap on the glass. He comes to the door, jingling a set of keys, and unlocks the deadbolt.

"Good," he says. "You changed your mind."

"About what?"

"Having your picture taken." He points to a photo of a young girl on the wall, a framed glossy. "I could put it there, only bigger."

"Maybe some other time."

"You sure?"

"I'm sure," I say. "I was hoping I could catch a ride home with you."

"Give me a minute to lock up," he says.

Earl drives a newer Firebird with wide tires and a T-top. The sky is dark now, and as we cruise down Hollywood Boulevard I look at the lighted marquees of the different theaters. The Egyptian. The Hollywood. The Pacific. I'm light-headed from the beer I drank at my brother's place and crave another. If one makes me feel good, a couple more will make me feel even better. I want to get drunk. I want to get sky-high drunk. There's no other reason to drink, since I don't care for the taste.

"Can you do me a favor?" I say.

"Like what?"

"Buy me a six-pack. I got the money."

He's quiet for a moment.

"I don't know," he says, shaking his head. "What are you, thirteen? Fourteen? That's awfully young to be drinking."

"I don't need a lecture," I say.

"No, I don't suppose you do. You seem pretty grown-up for your age. Where do you plan on drinking it?"

"At the park."

"That's not too smart."

"Who cares?"

"I just don't want you getting in trouble, because if you get in trouble that means I get in trouble. I don't need that. Tell you what," he says. "I'll buy you a six-pack but you have to drink at my place. It's not a good idea to be wandering around the park drunk, especially at night."

There's a liquor store on the corner down the block from our complex, and after Earl buys the beer we go up to his apartment. The first can goes down fast, and somewhere in there, as I'm working on my second, he reaches under the couch and pulls out the top of an old shoebox. In it is marijuana.

"Ever smoke weed?" he says.

I tell him I have, and it's true, though I've never much liked how it makes me feel. I prefer to drink but when he offers me the joint I take a few hits anyway to show that I'm cool. That I'm not afraid. It's powerful stuff. "From Maui," he says. "They call it Maui Wowwee." He laughs. On the TV is an old rerun of *Star Trek*, and while we're watching the good ship *Enterprise* weather a meteor attack he slides his hand along the back of the couch. I'm twelve years old but I am not stupid. I know what this is about. I know what's coming and I can't explain it away, saying I'm drunk and stoned, but it's as if I'm in another place at that moment, someplace far from here, that it's not me sitting on that couch beside Earl. He starts with my hair, lifting strands of it, then slowly growing bolder and holding them out as if he's measuring.

"You're beautiful," he says, and he says it softly.

I don't say anything. I don't move and he takes this as a sign and begins to stroke the side of my neck with the back of his hand. He raises my chin with the tips of his fingers as if posing me. "You really are beautiful," he says. "It's a shame you won't let me take your picture." Then he kisses my ear, and it feels good, feels gentle like a warm breeze. A chill passes through my body. He kisses me again, farther down my neck. I stand up. I start toward the door.

"Where you going?" he says. "Come here. I didn't mean to scare you."

But I am outside now in the hallway, and I hear other voices. I hear laughter. From over the railing I see my mother floating on her back in the pool, her eyes closed, her hair fanning out around her. My sister stands at the edge of the deep end, her arms stretched toward the sky, poised to dive. She looks up. She sees me. "Hey, Jimmy," she says. "Where you been?" Threads of light reflect beneath the surface of the water, twisting and bending, and when she dives they shatter into a million sparks. Dizzy, short of breath, I move toward the explosion of light.

DAISY

When I'm trying to patch things up, I buy my wife a present. Perfume maybe. A box of *See's* or her favorite peanut brittle. Later I'll take her out to dinner, apologize profusely and promise to treat her better. But my last binge was particularly loathsome, I feel particularly rotten about my drinking and drugging, and I want to do something special for her. She is a homemaker who collects little ceramic piggies, piggy salt and pepper shakers, stuffed animal piggies and china with piggies painted on them, and because she collects these pigs it occurs to me, in my hungover state of mind, that she might appreciate having the real thing.

I've heard her talk many times about the Vietnamese potbellied pig, how intelligent they are, even smarter than dogs, and what fine and affectionate pets they make. So that next day, after another night of heavy drinking, and while my wife is off running errands, I dig out the newspaper. I turn to the classifieds and find exactly what I'm looking for listed under Livestock: *Baby Potbellied Pigs. Wonderful pets. Registered. $150.00 & up.* The number has a desert area code. I dial it and a teenage boy answers.

"Yeah," he says.

"I saw your ad in the paper," I say. "About the potbellied pigs."

"Hang on," he says. Then I hear him holler, "Mom, you got any pigs left?" I can't make out her answer, the TV in the background is too loud, but a few seconds later he returns to the phone. "Yeah," he says, "we got one female left."

"Can you hold it for me?"

"First come, first serve," he says. "You want to know how to get here?"

"Let me grab a pen," I say.

Nature furnishes all of its creatures with a special ability to defend themselves against their predators. The deer, like the rabbit, boasts swiftness of foot and highly sensitive hearing. The bird possesses the gift of flight. The turtle has its bone-hard shell, the skunk a foul-smelling oily liquid. And the Vietnamese potbellied pig, a stout, short-legged mammal with bristly coarse hair, is blessed with a bloodcurdling, ear-piercing cry that paralyzes its enemies dead in their tracks. To the baby Vietnamese potbellied pig I purchase that afternoon for the outrageous sum of two hundred and fifty dollars, I am that enemy. I am that predator. The first time the teenage boy places that pig in my arms it lets out such a painfully high-pitched squeal that my ears ring for several minutes afterward. I am stunned. I am dazed. That at this point it is no bigger than a puppy, weighing no more than ten or twelve pounds, makes its powers all the more impressive. Imagine, I think, what it will sound like when it's all grown-up. This omen, how-ever, doesn't stop me from buying the little piglet, nor does the fact that I have yet to consider where we will keep it.

"How big do these things get?" I ask.

The boy shrugs.

"Hard to tell. All depends. We butcher the ones we don't sell at about eighty, ninety pounds. But this is the runt of the litter," he says. "I don't see her getting past sixty, tops."

To me the pig is a highly unattractive animal with beady eyes and chubby jowls and short bony legs far too thin to sup-port its enormous weight. It's a freak of nature. A bad joke from God. But the features I abhor in the Vietnamese potbel-lied pig, or any pig for that matter, are the very ones that my wife finds so appealing.

"Oh, how cute," she says, when I bring it home that

evening in a flimsy cardboard box. I set it on the living room floor. Her face softens, and I think I'm in the clear.

Upstairs, in the boys' bedroom, I hear the beeping and fake explosions of the Nintendo game they're playing. My wife kneels beside the box. She reaches in for the little pig.

"Better put cotton in your ears," I say. "That thing has one mean squeal."

In her arms, however, it doesn't let out a peep. Instead it burrows its snout into the warm flesh of her stomach and closes its beady eyes.

"You probably scared her," she says. "She's so sweet. Aren't you?" she says to the pig. "You're just a sweet little thing."

I'm pleased she likes it. Pleased that I did something good, something special to make up for the night before.

"Let me shower," I say, "and then I'll take you out to Papaguyo's. Have a couple margaritas. A good dinner."

"Why?"

"Why not?"

Her face hardens again. "You're an asshole, that's why not. You come home drunk at three in the morning, no calls, no nothing, and you expect me to be *nice*. I don't think so." She looks away from me in disgust and cuddles the pig. "Daisy," she says, cooing in its hairy little ear. "I think I'll name you Daisy."

When I think of a daisy I picture a flower with a yellow

center and white rays. I don't, by any stretch, see a pig with bristly black hair and stubby legs. But when I think of myself, I see her point. And part of me wants to change. To right my ways. The alcoholic, however, like the pig, is created with certain defense mechanisms and mine are denial and rage. They make for the better part of me, too, and I explode.

"Fuck it," I tell her. "Stay home with your stupid pig. I don't give a shit. But I'm going out. I'm getting wasted."

"So what's new?"

"Nothing," I say. "Nothing's ever new with us."

She holds the pig closer and it makes a soothing, grunting noise in her arms.

"Daisy," she says. "My sweet little Daisy."

I don't think anyone ever really knows why they get divorced or have affairs or regularly drink and drug themselves into a stupor. My memories of our last days together are splintered, lost in a haze of booze and dope, yet one thing remains absolutely clear. And that thing is Daisy. The measure of her growth is the final measure of my marriage: The fatter she gets, the worse my marriage seems to become.

I mean this literally.

Pound for pound. Blow for blow.

I am sitting on the floor in the basement. This is where I write. It is night and my wife and children have gone to bed. Daisy is asleep in her box in the kitchen above me and the house is quiet. Surrounding me are five neat piles of handwritten manuscript. I am struggling to get another novel off the ground. In fact, I am struggling to get five novels off the ground all at the same time and that's the problem. I can't focus. I can't make up my mind. This has been going on for months, long before Daisy's arrival, and I have sixty pages of one book, forty something of another. The others are shorter but they all have one thing in common: Each peters out, coincidentally, when the drugs wear off and I see them for what they are, these awful things I've written under the influence of methamphetamine and alcohol.

Tonight I am relatively sober. I've only drunk a few beers, and in terms of narcotics I haven't touched a thing in two miserable days. But trace amounts of meth are still coursing through my veins, and as I read over the first sentence of one of the five manuscripts I am far from clearheaded. On a notepad, in long hand only I can decipher, I write and rewrite that opening sentence nine different ways. I excogitate on a single word. I contemplate its deep symbolic meanings in relation to the profound themes of my work. I am brilliant. I am divinely inspired. Then I apply this divine inspiration to the opening lines of my other four manuscripts, believing that if I only concentrate long enough, hard enough, that some grand truth will soon reveal itself to me and I'll know, once and for all, which story most deserves the full attention of my genius. Only there's a short circuit somewhere in my brain. The traffic of ideas runs in circles, round and round, and then shoots off down a thousand different streets. I don't know which one to follow. I don't know which way to turn or where to get off and I'm on this crazy ride now when a piercing squeal, like the screech of brakes, brings the traffic in my head to a sudden standstill.

I am not, by nature, a mean or intolerant man. After all, she is still a piglet. At this point we've only had her a couple of weeks, and like a puppy you have to expect a certain amount of whining and crying. But we all have our limits, and when she squeals again, instead of losing my temper, I give in. I give up for the night and head upstairs to the kitchen. Her box is beside the stove so that the heat from the pilot lights will keep her warm and snug. But it's too small for her already, this box. Just the week before it was roomy and now she can hardly turn around in it. As of this morning Daisy weighs exactly twenty-nine and one-half pounds. I know this because I put her on the bathroom scale when it struck me how quickly she seemed to be growing.

We keep a big sack of piggy food in the pantry, and I fill her dish from it, these hard green pellets of compressed alfalfa. She makes loud slurping noises as she eats, and when she's done, which takes only a matter of seconds, she looks up at me with those beady little eyes and grunts for more.

"That's it," I say. "No more. Enough."

I turn off the kitchen light and feel my way through the dark to the bathroom. I brush my teeth. I wash my face and gargle twice. Then I go quietly into the bedroom, undress and slip under the covers beside my wife. It's maybe ten thirty, eleven o'clock at night. Her body is warm, and I curl up close. I take in the scent of her freshly shampooed hair.

"You awake?" I whisper.

"Not anymore."

I pass my hand along her thigh. The skin is soft and smooth. We haven't made love in over a month, and it's been like this, off and on now for a couple of years. She bats my hand away.

"Knock it off," she says.

"Honey," I say. "Baby, don't be like that."

"You reek," she says.

"I brushed my teeth. I gargled twice."

"It's inside you," she says. "The stink. All the booze and cigarettes and God knows whatever else you put in your body. It doesn't just wash off, you know. The whole room smells when you come to bed."

She rolls over on her side, away from me, and I think about getting up. I think about storming off and sleeping on the couch. Or down in the basement. I don't know why she stays with me, if it's about love for the man she remembers, the one long before the drugs and alcohol really took hold, or if instead it's about fear. Fear of having to strike out on her own with three kids in tow and not many marketable skills. That Heidi doesn't drink or drug places the burden of our failed marriage squarely on my shoulders. I just lie there in bed, without any answers, staring at the ceiling until my eyes grow heavy.

It's hard, if not impossible, for some people to fall asleep when they're mad, but it's like anything else. Practice makes perfect, and pretty soon, if you do it enough, it comes like second nature. Of course that next morning we wake up angry, and to compound that anger, when I pour myself a cup of coffee and head down to the basement to get back to work, I find my manuscripts—the manuscripts I'd left neatly stacked on the floor—chewed and mauled beyond recognition. All of them. Destroyed. Bits and pieces of paper are everywhere. Slowly I take a deep breath. Slowly I exhale. I call for her, sweetly, so she'll come out from hiding.

"Daisy. Little Daisy, where are you?"

But my wife, who woke first this morning, is a step ahead of me. She is standing in the doorway, cuddling the pig to her chest.

"She got out of her box last night," she says.

"I can see that."

I start toward her.

"Give her to me," I say.

She steps back, holding the pig tighter. "Don't even think about it." Then she looks at the scraps of paper strewn all over the floor. She laughs. "You'll never finish another novel anyway. Face it, honey, you're all washed up."

I would like to think that I am not alone in my resentment toward the pig. I would like to believe that I have allies in my two sons, Andy and Logan, ages ten and six, respectively, but unfortunately this is not the case. Like their mother, the boys take to Daisy as they would to a new puppy. They enjoy petting its ugly coarse hair as they would a smooth coat of fur. They enjoy laughing while it gorges itself, devouring its meals and all our table scraps in record time. They enjoy playing with it and chasing it around the house and making it squeal until I think my head is about to explode. But what they do not enjoy is cleaning up the piggy litter box, and since their mother is also of little help in this matter, the chore is frequently left to me. For the good of the family, as Daisy's appetite grows, it becomes increasingly clear to everyone that she must be relocated. It's a rare occasion but for once we are all in complete agreement.

Soon after the manuscript episode, I drive down to Home Depot and buy enough wood, wire and nails to build her a nice pen in our backyard. The cost is ninety-three dollars. To shelter piggy from the elements, I also build her a nice house. It's a large house, too, and the materials set me back another twenty-eight. Counting the two fifty I paid for her, along with the vet bill for her shots, another forty-five, I am now into Daisy for four hundred and sixteen dollars, not including the cost of piggy food.

That night after I build the pen and piggy house, between the hours of ten o'clock and five in the morning, I rest soundly believing I have solved at least one of the problems in my marriage. At exactly 5:03 A.M., however, that belief—like my manuscripts—is torn to shreds. Daisy is banging on her gate, demanding to be fed. For this she uses her snout, repeatedly ramming it against the gate until she wakes me from a deep sleep.

I throw open the window.

Our backyard is small and her pen is just a few yards from our bedroom. It's dawn and I can see her beady little eyes staring up at me in the growing light. She snorts. She grunts.

"No," I shout. "Bad girl. Bad Daisy."

For a while, say a week, this approach works, and I'm able to fall quickly back to sleep. But it's a process of diminishing returns, and soon the mild admonitions of "no" and "bad girl" escalate into threats along the lines of "shut the fuck up." The pig, however, no longer fears me, she hasn't for some time, and the more I holler, the louder the banging seems to get. Daisy is taunting me. Daisy is egging me on.

As usual my wife just rolls over in bed. Somehow it never seems to bother her. I don't understand it.

"That pig," I tell her, "is driving me crazy."

"You bought her."

"I thought you'd like it."

"I do. You're the one with the problem. You're the one who keeps waking me every morning with all your stupid screaming. Grow up. It's a pig and that's what they live for. *Food.* That's what they do. *Eat.*"

I know she's right. The pig is only doing what pigs do best, and as an alcoholic I should understand this far better than most—the nature of obsession, of compulsion, the constant quest for more when there can never be enough. But having knowledge and using it are two vastly different matters. So that morning, spent and frustrated from hollering, as I lie in bed listening to Daisy banging at the gate, I come up with a simple but surefire plan: stack rocks in front of it. Big rocks.

Like a stone fence.

That same morning, with my head pounding and my mouth chalky and dry, I find myself hauling rocks up from the creek that runs alongside our house. It's a hard job, and I break a good sweat. I also slip once and fall into the creek, tearing a hole in a new pair of Levi's and cutting my hand.

Soaked, sweating and bleeding, I stand in the pigpen and

look at my handiwork. Six heavy rocks, around thirty pounds each, are strategically positioned between Daisy and the gate.

"Now bang on it, bitch."

I smile.

One of the rocks is smeared with my blood. At first Daisy just sniffs at it. She doesn't know what it is. Then her tongue darts out and suddenly her beady little eyes spring open and she's wild, grunting and snorting, sniffing the rocks for more of my blood.

Each day the pen grows a little smaller. Each day the nice roomy house I made for her is a little less nice and roomy. Inside of a month she can barely squeeze into it and her ass sticks out the door. That part I like—her discomfort.

"You should've anticipated this," my wife says. "Look at the poor thing. She can't even move. You need to build a bigger house."

"I will."

"When?"

"Tomorrow. I promise."

"Where have I heard that before?"

My wife is referring to my drinking and my repeated vows to quit. In my hungover state of mind, I don't care to discuss it.

"Forget it," she says, waving me off. "I'll just buy one."

And she does. It's one of those igloo-style doghouses that they sell at Home Depot and it sets us back another eighty-seven bucks. The total outlay for Daisy rises to five hundred and three dollars, not including the cost of piggy food, which has gone up considerably. Eight days after the manuscript massacre I weigh her again and she comes in at an even fifty-four pounds. Two weeks later it's ninety-eight. By the end of that month she's topping a hundred and ten, and I get on the phone. I call that kid who sold her to me and he denies everything.

"I don't know where you got your information," he says, "but it wasn't me. They average about a hundred and fifty. That's when we butcher them anyway, the ones we don't sell. You want, we'll take her back."

I know exactly what he'd do. The idea strikes me as a good one.

"Let me think about it," I tell him, and then I hang up.

As Daisy continues to grow, so do her muscles. Her neck is as thick and strong as a linebacker's, and with it she is soon able to move heavy rocks. I discover this at five in the morning when I'm awakened from a deep sleep. I throw open the bedroom window. I look into the pen. In the dawn's light she is prying with her snout, lifting with her neck, banging one of the rocks against the gate. She does this repeatedly. To taunt me. There can be no other explanation.

She pulls her snout out from under the rock. Stares up at me. Grunts.

"It ain't over yet," I say.

My wife wakes.

"Who you talking to?"

"Nobody," I say. "I must've had a nightmare."

Later that afternoon, on my way home from work, I stop off at Home Depot again and buy a bag of spiked plates. Each is three by five inches and boasts twenty-four razor-sharp points. Typically they're used for joining rafters in rough frame construction, but I mount them on the opposite side of the gate, leaving the treacherous spikes exposed. Pigs have extremely poor eyesight, and so I mount them just before dark. I mount them while she's distracted, devouring her evening meal. I want it to be a surprise.

"Eat up," I say. "Enjoy."

Where my initial reprimands succeeded in quieting Daisy for about a week, and the rocks nearly a month, the spikes fail miserably from the very beginning. The difference is that I'm not asleep this time. For most of the night I lie awake, partly because I'm worried about things—my marriage, my children, my writing and drinking—and partly because I'm excited. I want to be awake for this. I want to experience the moment— that bloodcurdling squeal when she first encounters the spikes. But at five that morning, instead of a painful squeal, I hear the banging of the gate again. I get out of bed and go to the window. In the dawn's early light, Daisy is rubbing her rump against the spikes as if she's simply scratching an itch. At this point I snap.

I put on my pants. I put on a shirt and a pair of shoes and hurry quietly outside to the storage cabinet. This is where we keep our household chemicals, half-empty buckets of paint, cans of lacquer thinner, wood stain, quarts of motor oil and a spare gallon of gasoline in a red can. I carry the red can around to the backyard. I empty out a spray bottle of window cleaner and refill it with gas and walk calmly over to the pigpen. The sun is rising, and I can see clearly now. I can see everything clearly now. I know what I must do and I am not thinking of my children or my wife and how my actions might endanger them.

"Daisy," I say. "C'mere, Daisy. I have a little surprise."

I hold the bottle up to her snout. Immediately she recoils.

"Like that?" I say. "Huh? It smell good?"

I spray the rocks with it. I spray the spikes and the gate and the dirt all around it. Then I start back into the house, confident that I've solved the problem, if only temporarily, when I hear something that stops me dead in my tracks. At first I can't make out what it is, or maybe it's that I can't believe it, but I hear it again. These wet slurping noises. Slowly I turn around.

She is licking at the rocks.

She is lapping at the spikes. That's how I lose it. My mind. I walk back to the pen. I squat down. Face-to-face. Pig to man.

"Like it?" I say. "Gas? This good gas? Want some more?"

Daisy glares at me with those beady little eyes and snorts. I lower the nozzle. I slip my finger around the trigger and I'm just about to squeeze down on it when my wife calls to me from our bedroom window.

"What're you doing?"

"Nothing, honey."

"What's that smell?"

"What smell?"

"It's gas. I smell gas."

She sees the red can that I set nearby on the ground. Then she looks at the bottle in my hand.

"My God," she screams, "is that what you're spraying? Are you trying to kill the poor thing? Are you trying to burn down the house? You're sick," she says. "You're out of your fucking mind."

She threatens to call the Humane Society. She says something about calling the cops, too, but I don't stick around to see if she'll follow through. I take refuge at a local bar and wallow in my anger, an anger that has been building now for some time. Like an ugly hangover, it carries over from one day to the next, and eventually I don't think my wife and I even know what we're fighting about anymore. We fight, I guess, because the anger is never resolved and we're unaware of it, how left unchecked it only grows, how that anger turns to resentment, that resentment into coldness. A bitter coldness. The kind that kills.

A storm has moved in this morning. It's pouring outside and the place is packed with construction workers taking advantage of their day off. The guy beside me has a cigarette dangling from his lips. He's patting his pockets for his lighter, and I hand him mine. I strike up a conversation. I tell him about the pig, not the whole story, just parts. In no time he's laughing.

"My brother-in-law had one of those," he says. "Lived twenty-two years. Weighed two hundred and fifty pounds. They're tough fuckers, you know, from the jungles of Vietnam."

Twenty-two years.

I roll those words over in my head. Twenty-two more years of this and I will be an old man. I will be full of contempt and self-loathing. Our children will be grown and gone. Without them, my wife and I will become one of those bitter old couples who have their own bedrooms and only talk to each other when they have to. Crippled with regret and remorse, we will push on gallantly, battling it out to the bitter end.

The bartender approaches.

"Another drink?" he asks.

"Why not?" I say.

He looks at me and sniffs the air.

"Do you smell gas?"

"No," I say. "But something around here definitely stinks."

I'm not sure when I return home. What happens once I get a few drinks in me is that I want something more, and once I get that something more there's no stopping me. I'm off and running. Generally my binges don't last longer than three or four days, and because it's still storming when I run out of money, drugs and booze, I'm guessing that, at most, only a night or two has passed.

I run out of gas about a mile from my house and have to walk the rest of the way. It's late at night and cold. The rain is coming down hard. My clothes are soaked and I'm chilled to the bone. When I last slept, I don't know, but I am weak with fatigue. What I need is another drink, some clean dry clothes, a warm bed. I stagger across the driveway and pull myself up the porch steps. For a while I lean against the hand railing, struggling to catch my breath, then I fumble for my house key. I try to slip it into the lock. I try several times before I realize that it no longer fits. Suddenly I'm enraged. I pound on the door. I shout for her. I shout for my children but no one answers.

A light glows in the living room. The curtains are drawn but there's a space between them, and when I stumble into the flower bed to look through the window, I see Daisy sprawled in my La-Z-Boy, one hoof hanging over the armrest. She is staring at the TV, the screen flickering with static.

PERSONAL EFFECTS

My brother is standing outside the baggage claim dressed like a cop. This wouldn't be unusual if that's what he did for a living, police work, but it's not. Barry is an actor and sometimes he just doesn't know when to stop. I pull to the curb and tap the horn. He looks through the traffic, spots me, waves. We're at the airport in San Jose and I've come to pick him up. I've come to take him to see our father who was taken to the hospital the night before.

I'm driving the old man's truck, and it's a tired one, a real workhorse. There's no radio or heater and it won't go into second gear anymore, but it's served our father well through the years and I like it. How it rides bumpy. How you have to wrestle the wheel when you make a turn. My brother climbs into the front seat and I put it into first gear. He doesn't look good. He's gained too much weight, his face is bloated and his eyes are dull. But I don't say anything. I give it some gas and we go.

"How's he holding up?" he asks.

"He's doing okay."

"What do the doctors say?"

"They never tell you much. I don't think they know much or they won't let on. But they moved him out of intensive care this morning."

"That's a good sign," he says.

Our father, he had a stroke. I called Barry with the news after our stepmother called me and that's why we're here. I took the Greyhound in from San Francisco. Barry flew in from L.A., just off the set with a small role in a B movie called *Piranha*. Our sister, she has a little girl to look after and can't make it on short notice. She lives in L.A., too.

"What's with the uniform?" I say.

He lifts the badge from his chest with the tips of his fingers and smiles.

"Looks real, doesn't it?" he says.

"You know you can get in serious trouble going around like that."

A plane roars by overhead, the noise almost deafening.

When it passes I look over at my brother again and try to smile. But it's a forced smile because he worries me. He's worried me for a while now. His drinking has progressed rapidly over the last few years. "I didn't have any clean clothes," he says. "And I didn't have time to do the wash. That all right with you?" he says. "I just got your call and jumped on the plane." He reaches around to his back pocket and takes out a half-pint wrapped in a brown paper bag and offers it to me. I wave it off. It's only about ten o'clock and already he is drunk or well on his way. Sometimes it's hard to tell if he's truly drunk, because he drinks so much and because he's so good at maintaining. I've seen him put away a fifth and not slur his words or weave when he walks. But the smell, you can't hide that. It fills the inside of the truck and I crack my window and let in some fresh air. He takes a drink and caps the bottle and rests it between his legs.

"A couple nights ago," he says, "I was driving home from the set and this woman cut me off. We're on the Hollywood Freeway and when she exits I follow her off the ramp. I pull up alongside her while we're stopped at the red light and flash her my badge. 'Hey, lady,' I say, 'I could give you a ticket for cutting me off back there.' " He laughs. " 'But I'll let you off with a warning this time. Just don't let it happen again.' "

He laughs harder. It's his trademark laugh, a high-pitched laugh that I've always enjoyed, and it makes me want to laugh with him. But I don't find the story so funny. I also don't believe it. My brother likes to embellish. He likes to make up stories, and sometimes it worries me. Sometimes I wonder if he knows the difference between the truth and a lie.

This is June and we're in the middle of a heat wave. Yesterday it hit a hundred degrees before noon, and today doesn't promise to be any kinder. The sun is beating through the windshield, and while we're stopped for a light I notice that he's sweating, heavily, like he's sick with fever. The ends of his hair are soaked and he keeps wiping his forehead with the back of his arm. "Doesn't this thing have air-conditioning?" he says, and I want to tell him that it wouldn't matter. That what he needs to do is quit drinking or at the very least cut back to just beer and wine. I have a few myself every other day, and though on weekends I don't usually bother to keep count, I believe that I am perfectly fine. I believe that I am far from becoming anything like my brother. But I tell him none of these things, and when the light changes I put the truck into gear and start across the intersection and onto the freeway.

As we drive toward the hospital I look out over the valley. Where there were once apricot orchards, orange groves and wide-open fields, now all you see are housing tracts, strip malls, gas stations, fast-food places. We talk about this, my brother and I, how it's all changed since we were children. We talk about the house that our father built for us and lost. We talk about the older San Jose, downtown, and how it's blighted now, the different shops and stores all boarded up because people prefer the malls in the suburbs. We talk about anything but the man responsible for our being here on this hot morning in June in this beat-up old truck.

Even at the hospital, as we ride the elevator up to see our father, we talk about other things. Barry tells me that he has to move out of his house in Echo Park. He has until the end of the month.

"After that," he says, "I don't know what I'll do. Maybe Marilyn will let me stay with her until I get back on my feet."

"You can live with me."

I mean it, and when he doesn't say anything I find myself suddenly angry.

"Fuck Hollywood," I say. "You need to get out of that place and sober up."

The elevator doors open. We step out and start down the hall, looking at the numbers on the doors. Our father is in room 614. "Did you hear me?" I say. We pass room 609. We pass 610 and 611 and he still hasn't answered. It could be that he's seriously mulling over the offer. It could be that he's mad at me because I told him the truth. I don't know. I don't know if I have ever understood my brother. We are inside room 614 now, where our father lies, his eyes half closed, drowsing, with a tube running from one arm and wires connected to his chest.

I am scared for him. I am worried. But as we approach the bed I am thinking, oddly, only of my brother.

Strokes often come in pairs. Where the first is mild, the second can be fatal. And the chances of another striking are greatest in the first forty-eight hours. Beyond keeping the patient calm and relaxed as possible, and monitoring his vitals, there is little the doctors can do. But hope is on our father's side and he does not suffer that second stroke, the one that kills. Unfortunately the first has robbed him of the use of his right hand, he can hardly open and close it, and for someone who has made his living all of his life working with his hands this is a particularly devastating blow.

After three days the doctors send him home to his wife, Aileen, our former baby-sitter, along with a prescription for blood thinner and a rubber ball that he is supposed to practice squeezing. The idea is to rebuild the muscles of his hand, to somehow retrain them. "It's the mind-body connection," he tells us, when we're back at the house. We have been back for a few hours now and we're sitting around the kitchen table with a bottle of Canadian Club. It's late in the afternoon and the drapes are drawn to help keep out the heat. Our father is wearing Bermuda shorts and his favorite Hawaiian shirt and I think that this is good, not to have to see him in that ugly hospital gown. Except for being a little pale, a little shaken for the experience, he seems fine. The hand, you can't tell anything is wrong by looking. He is squeezing the ball as we drink, or trying to anyway. The fingers will barely move.

"What's it feel like?" Barry says.

"It's strange," he says. "When you will it to move and it won't."

Barry is wearing the pants to his uniform but he's stripped down to his T-shirt. The alcohol is making him sweat again, and I would like to think our father would notice, that it's a sign too obvious to deny. I am surprised then, when he smiles at Barry from across the table and tells him that he looks good. Healthy. That he must be working out. They haven't seen each other for months, not since Christmas, and in that time my brother's drinking has clearly escalated. It shows in his face, in the bloat, in the dull bloodshot eyes. But then I am no one to talk. I am no one to judge. I am drinking right along with them, shot for shot, when our stepmother comes into the kitchen. She's been out shopping and is carrying a big bag of groceries. She sets it on the counter, looks at our father and shakes her head.

"Don," she says, "what do you think you're doing?"

"*Mi vida*," he says. "*No más un poquito.*"

"A little, my ass," she says. "You know you're not supposed to drink on your medication." But he gives her a smile, and she softens. She shakes her head again. "A few hours out of the hospital," she says, "and already you're acting like nothing happened. I can't leave you bums alone for a minute."

"C'mon, pull up a chair."

"I don't know about you," she says.

"Have a drink. Jimmy," he says, "you want to make her a drink, a screwdriver."

"Just one," she says, and she means it.

So I make her a drink, a screwdriver, and for a while it's like old times, sitting around the kitchen table with my brother and father getting wasted on a hot afternoon. The liquor has taken effect and I dismiss my concerns as petty and hypocritical. Barry will be fine. This is just a phase he's going through. And our father, he'll be all right, too. There is no reason to worry. We are just men doing what men do when they drink. We tell tall stories. We get loud sometimes. Or too sentimental. We solve world problems and make big plans and promises to each other that we will never keep.

I am the youngest and I am proud that I can keep up with my father and brother. I am proud for the liquor I can hold. But we all have our limits, and soon after dinner the room begins to spin. I go into the guest room and lie down on the bed and shut my eyes. That only makes it worse, and I think I'm going to be sick, but it subsides, and a short while later I pass out.

When I wake up the room is dark. Someone has taken off

my shoes and covered me with a blanket. My throat is dry, I can hardly swallow. I get up from the bed slowly, because my head is pounding, and wander into the kitchen for a glass of water. It has to be around two or three in the morning and the house is quiet except for the hum of the refrigerator. I pour myself a glass of water, drink it and pour another. I'm so dehydrated that I can't seem to get enough. On my way back to bed I notice that there's a light on in the living room, and I walk toward it. I pause in the hallway. He is sitting in an armchair under the dim light of the table lamp with a drink at his side. He is reading a book. I do not know what book. But in the shadows of the light the bloat in his face seems to have disappeared and his eyes are clear and sharp. He looks up at me and smiles and in that moment I see him again, the old Barry, healthy and untroubled. Then he turns slightly, more toward the light and the picture changes. Something about the smile isn't right. I don't know what exactly, or how to describe it, but it looks almost as if it hurts him. It looks as if he's doing it for my sake, on cue, like he might for the camera, and inside him I can sense something tightening, something closing down and pulling us further apart.

I live in a dirty little beach town called Pacifica, about ten miles south of San Francisco. It is foggy all year round, but on those rare days when the sky is clear I can look out the window and watch the waves rise and break along the beach. My place is small, just one room and a kitchenette, and I don't have a couch. I don't have any armchairs or even a TV set. But I do have a table to eat on. I do have a desk and a typewriter and a bed to sleep in and for now, as a college student at San Francisco State, that's all I need. For now, as an alcoholic, that is all my brother needs, a place where he can stay and dry out, and where at night, when you close your eyes, you can hear the waves breaking in the distance.

I sit down to write him a letter the night after I return from San Jose. In it I want to tell him that I admire him for his accomplishments, his drive and ambition. At twenty-seven he has already worked in over forty television shows and starred in two movies, *Bad Company* with Jeff Bridges and *Daisy Miller* with Cybill Shepherd. You should be proud, I want to say. You didn't know anybody when we first moved to L.A. and in a few short years you're a contract player for Universal taking home five hundred dollars a week. That's not bad for a kid. And it was just the beginning. But things changed. You started drinking too much and hanging out with some fucked-up people. I'd like to blame them. I'd like to blame Hollywood and all it stands for but I know it's not that simple—that blame isn't even what it's about. What matters now, and this is *all* that matters, is that you straighten up or you're no good for anyone, especially yourself.

Look, I want to say.

Take a good hard look.

You haven't worked in three years except for this lousy role in a low-budget movie, a role you never would've taken if you hadn't needed the money, and you have to ask yourself why. What brought you here? Don't blame it on bad luck. Don't blame it on a bad childhood. I'd like you to come stay with me for a while. I think you need to get away from Hollywood, and when you're strong again, when you're ready, you can always go back.

These are the things I want to tell my brother, and I do. They aren't the exact words—I can't remember what I actually wrote—but the sentiment is the same, and I sent the letter off the next morning on my way to school. About a week later I get a phone call. It's close to midnight, and he's drunk again.

"I got your letter," he says, "and you're right, man. I have to do something because I'm going nowhere but down and I can't stop it. I mean the drinking. I can't fucking stop. Every morning I wake up, I say 'Today I won't drink. Today I will be sober.' Then my head starts pounding and my hands start shaking and I sink into this deep depression, this deep dark ugly depression. It's a horrible place," he says, "and it's killing me. I know that. But it's killing me if I *don't* drink."

I'm convinced that it will pass—the depression, the fears. I'm convinced that I can make the difference. We talk for well over an hour.

We work things out.

Here is our plan: Final exams begin for me next week but as soon as they end, on Friday, I will borrow our father's truck and drive down to Los Angeles that same night. We'll take as many of his things as we can in one trip and store the rest in Marilyn's garage or give them away to the Salvation Army. Of course we'll need to bring his bed, because I only have the one. And having his couch would be nice, if we can fit it onto the truck. I'm excited discussing the details. I think we're both excited with the prospect of living together again, of making a fresh start. From that point on there will be no more drinking. I will quit with him in moral support, quit my own balancing act between drinking and studying. Every morning, where before Barry would wake up hungover and immediately reach for a drink, I will make him coffee and a good breakfast. Later we will run on the beach. Maybe we will join a gym. We will sweat the toxins out of his system and soon the bloat will vanish. His eyes will clear. At night we will relax and take long walks or fish off the pier or go to a movie, and it won't be easy, I understand this, but in time his depression will lift and the compulsion to drink will pass and I will have him back, the brother I remember.

"Friday," I say.

"Friday," he says, just before we hang up. "I'll see you next Friday."

But of course that Friday never comes. On Tuesday of the following week, three days before I was to leave for Los Angeles, I get a phone call from my stepmother. It's around four o'clock in the morning, and I'm up, wired on No Doz and coffee. I'm cramming for finals.

"Jimmy," she says. "You need to come over as soon as possible."

"What happened?"

"Just come over," she says.

"Is it my dad? Is he all right?"

"He's okay," she says. "But he needs you right now. It's your brother," she says. She says, "He shot himself."

On the darker stretches of Highway 101 I feel motionless. Like the truck is not moving. Like I am standing still, fixed in time. Ahead only a small patch of road is illuminated by the headlamps, and behind me, when I glance into the rearview mirror, it's just darkness. Fog has settled over the highway, and the glare, the bright whiteness reflected in the lights, is blinding. I drive slowly and hope that the fog will lift soon. I listen to the engine, the rhythm of the pistons rising and falling, and do and do not think of my brother. He comes to me in flashes, his image stirring as if from a pool of still water, breaking the surface momentarily and then submerging again.

Beside me on the seat is a pint of vodka, and I sip from it

as I drive, trying to make it last. I don't want to be inside my head. I do not want to have to feel. I do not want to have to think. These are some of the reasons why my brother drank, and why, when the alcohol no longer worked, when it became a problem greater than the problems he drank to escape, he found another way. I would like to respect his decision. I would like to forgive him. But these things are not possible for me and I can't see how they ever will be. I take a drink and stare into the fog. I light a cigarette and roll down my window. The air that rushes in is cool and smells of salt and rotting seaweed, and I know, because the ocean is near, that I don't have much farther to go. I am returning to Los Angeles for my brother's funeral. I am returning to Los Angeles to claim the things that the dead leave for the living.

It has been less than a month since our father had his stroke, and on his doctor's advice he is not making this trip with me. But I believe that the real reason has less to do with matters of health than those of shame for a son who has taken his own life. The fog lifts when I pass Ventura Beach and turn inland and soon the traffic thickens. The night air grows warmer and instead of the salt and seaweed it smells vaguely of exhaust now. I get off the freeway in Studio City and cross an overpass that runs high above that concrete channel called the L.A. River. From there it's just a few blocks to my sister's place, and when I pull into the driveway I see that she's left the porch

light on for me. It's late, maybe two in the morning, and I fig-
ure she and her husband are asleep. The house key is supposed
to be under the mat, that was the arrangement so I wouldn't
have to wake them, but I don't have to use it. Marilyn greets me
on the front porch, we hold each other tightly, and in the dim
light I can see that her eyelids are red and swollen. "Oh God,"
she says. "Tell me this isn't happening." But I can tell her no
such thing. She is by nature timid and shy, she has always felt
too much too intensely, and I worry for her. I worry that this
is something from which she will never recover, and I worry for
myself, too, because we are very much the same.

He's dead, I want to say.

I want to say those words over and over to take the power
out of them, but I say nothing. I hold my sister for a while
longer and then we go inside. Her husband makes us drinks
and sets out a mirror, a razor and a straw on the coffee table.
We do not talk about Barry. Not a word. The funeral is to-
morrow morning and we ride out these last hours by numbing
ourselves with vodka, Valium and cocaine. The combination is
potent, and with the cocaine we are able to drink far past the
point where we might ordinarily pass out. We drink and drug
until the living room windows begin to fill with the morning
light, and my little niece wanders in on us, rubbing the sleep
from her eyes. She is wearing jumper pajamas. Her father hides
the mirror on a shelf above the stereo and my sister rises un-

steadily to her feet. "Munchikin," she says. "My little munchikin. C'mere, give me a hug." But my little niece hesitates, she looks away, and when she does step into her mother's open arms it is with a certain awkwardness. She is only three years old, and though she has no understanding of death or of the drugs we are using, she senses that things are not right.

"You better get her dressed," her father says. "The sitter will be here soon."

When they leave the room he pours us another drink, and later, in the car, we all do another line. I am impressed that he is able to drive so well. I am impressed that he is able to drive at all, or that he doesn't get us lost. Our only mistake is that in our fucked-up state of mind we don't think to leave the house early enough, and by the time we arrive the services are already under way. This is at Forest Lawn in Hollywood, and it is our mother's choice, for a funeral befitting an actor, to hold the services here where the stars are buried. She is sitting in the front pew with her new husband, ironically a Mormon from Utah, and my sister, her husband and I take seats in the back.

The chapel is small. There are maybe thirty, forty people present, and on a stand up front, near the podium, rests our brother's casket. The priest wears a solemn expression on his face and talks of Barry as if they had been intimate friends when in fact they had never known each other. As he drones on our mother rocks back and forth in her seat, keening. Then a strange thing happens to me. Their voices seem to fade. They grow fainter and fainter until I'm only watching their mouths work, and I suddenly feel very small. I watch the funeral play out in front of me but it's as if I'm viewing it all from a long distance, like you might in a dream. None of it is really happening, and I am somewhere else now. I am somewhere very far away.

It is an old house in a neighborhood of Echo Park that is not safe to walk at night. The paint is chipping off the sides and the shingles on the roof are cracked and brittle from the sun. The lawn is dry and yellow. There are no hedges or trees, no shade or cover, and if you stare long enough you can see waves of heat rising off the asphalt in the driveway. His car is still parked there, an old battered Volkswagen squatting on its axles, the backseat packed with boxes of books and clothes that he had planned to move, throw out or give away. The registration tag is nearly two years old.

On the front porch is an upturned wicker chair with the weaving broken out of the seat, and on the door is a warning from the Los Angeles city coroner: *Removal of this seal is a felony.* The day is hot, and I am sweating. The Fourth of July is near, and as I reach for the doorknob, turn it and find it unlocked, I hear the snap of firecrackers from somewhere down the block. For some time I have contemplated this moment, wondering if

I could go through with it, and I'm surprised at how easily I enter, without hesitation, without a second thought. The odor is overpowering. Immediately my throat tightens, and in that instant I want to turn back, but I do not. On a table in the hallway, just past the door, is a stack of unopened mail, and in the living room cardboard boxes are scattered across the floor. Some he has already packed but most are still empty. I'd like to think that he was preparing to move in with me. I'd like to believe that I could've helped if he'd given me the chance. But my sister tells me that he never mentioned anything about moving in with me and instead had borrowed money from her and rented a room in a run-down hotel in Hollywood not far from where he used to live, when he was just a teenager, when he first moved out.

I walk slowly through the house. A pile of neatly folded towels rests on the couch, and nearby, on the coffee table, is a basket of clean clothes still in need of sorting. The police uniform, the clothes I last saw him wearing, is among them.

I don't have to go far.

I don't have to search.

The living room adjoins the dining room and that is where he killed himself. I don't know why but he had dragged the box spring and mattress from his bedroom into this room, set up the nightstand, a reading lamp and portable fan. Maybe it was cooler here. Maybe it was only late at night, long after the sun had gone down, that my brother was able to sleep. I sit on the edge of the mattress. The pillow is dark and heavy with blood. There is still the indentation where he had rested his head.

On the floor beside the bed is an empty fifth of Kessler's, and I imagine him lifting it to his lips, draining the last of it before reaching for the revolver that he'd bought for home protection several years before. I imagine that the reading lamp is on but that it barely lights the room and that the fan is purring, turning back and forth, back and forth. Outside, maybe, he hears a car pass along the street. Maybe a dog is barking. I see him pull the drapes shut and stretch out on the bed. For a while he just lies there, staring at the ceiling. Does he think of me? Can he see the faces of our sister, father and mother? He places the barrel of the revolver in his mouth. He cocks the hammer. Where is he, in that instant between life and death, when he pulls the trigger? Somewhere down the block I hear more firecrackers go off, and I see him then, recoiling from the blast.

Sometimes late at night I will wake up in a cold sweat, unable to catch my breath. Sometimes when I am playing with my children, teaching class or talking with a friend, that scene will visit me. I could be reading the newspaper. I could be watching TV. I could be wasted or sober and suddenly I'm there again, just a college kid, sitting on the edge of that bed in that house in Echo Park where my brother ended his life. Now I'm forty-three years old, a middle-aged writer, and whenever I drive into Los Angeles on business, or to visit a friend, it fills me with a sense of dread. On every street, around every corner, I come face-to-face with the memory of my brother. Bronson Park. A restaurant on Sunset Boulevard where he once took me for lunch. Laurel Canyon where he lived in better times. Larry Edmund's Books in Hollywood. They are different moments but they all lead to the same place. There is no answer for suicide, no final reconciliation.

That afternoon in July I load our father's truck with my brother's belongings and vow never to return to Los Angeles. On Highway 101, while I'm driving along the coast smoking a cigarette and staring blankly out the window, I notice a sign up ahead. It's for the Pismo Beach turnoff, and seeing it I recall the day when our mother left our father and first moved us to L.A. We stopped here along the way to play in the ocean and have our picture snapped by a stranger. We are just children, my brother and sister and I, posing for the photo in front of an older Buick Special, squinting against the glare of the sun. He has his arm draped over Marilyn's shoulders, and later, in the car when I begin to cry, my brother will hold me and whisper something into my ear, something that will make me smile.

ON SELLING A NOVEL
TO HOLLYWOOD

DEAL I

I am twenty-eight years old, confident and self-assured. When Warner Brothers options my second novel I am ecstatic. In a year or so they'll make the movie and I will join the ranks of the rich and famous. Because the movie will be a phenomenal success, my novel will rocket to the top of the best-seller list. I will appear on all the big talk shows. My face will grace the cover of *Esquire*. Above all the *New Yorker* will finally stop rejecting my short stories and recognize me for the brilliant talent that I am. In the meantime the celebration begins. I run out and buy an eight-ball of coke, a few cases of Heineken, a half-gallon of Jack Daniel's, Absolut and Johnnie Walker Black and invite all my friends over for a party. The last guest leaves at dawn but I'm just getting started.

The novel I sold is about three teenage brothers growing up in some seedy parts of Los Angeles with their widowed mother. The oldest brother is an aspiring actor. The middle brother deals cocaine and methamphetamine. The youngest is a habitual runaway. They are poor kids. They are reckless kids on a collision course with life, and because I have lived this life, because I know these characters intimately, I want to write the screenplay.

I meet with the producer at Warner Brothers. At the main gate that afternoon is a long line of cars waiting for the guard to check them through. Ahead of me are a Mercedes, two BMWs and a Porsche. I am driving an eleven-year-old Nissan pickup with a broken muffler, and it's loud. People are staring at me and I'm suddenly self-conscious. On a whim I put it into reverse, and instead of parking on the studio lot as I was instructed to do, I leave my old truck at a meter down the street and walk back to the guard's booth. He passes me through, and a few minutes later I'm in an air-conditioned bungalow seated across from the producer and his assistant, an attractive girl who barely seems out of her teens. She's wearing a tight skirt and a low-cut blouse. The producer is in his early forties, fit and tanned. He is beginning to lose his hair.

"It's a terrific book," he says. "But I'm a little concerned. Novelists are generally too close to their own work to make the necessary changes."

"What kind of changes?" I say.

He waves his hand.

"Nothing major," he says. "We don't want to lose your vision of the story."

As we discuss these changes the assistant takes notes. She gets us coffee and Cokes and phones in lunch. She is very accommodating, and I wonder if she's just a good employee or if the producer is fucking her. On the wall behind the producer's desk are glossies of old movie stars. Bogart. Jimmy Stewart. Jane Russell. Now and then I glance at these photos while we talk, and now and then, though I know better, I steal a look at the assistant. Once she catches my eye and smiles.

When our meeting is over I leave the office determined to do a good job. I am prepared to be merciless. I am prepared to cut and chop. To rearrange scenes, create new ones, eliminate others. I work long hard hours and in three months I've whittled a three-hundred-page novel down to a hundred-and-ten-page screenplay. But the heart of the book is still there. All the characters survive intact.

"You certainly know how to write a screenplay," the producer tells me after he's read it. "But it's too dark. I think we need a fresh eye on this."

In short, I am fired and a fresh eye is hired. In this writer's version the oldest brother, the aspiring actor, is now the lead singer of a rock band. The middle brother is the bass guitarist.

The youngest, the runaway, is the drummer. They aren't tough kids anymore. They aren't even poor.

That writer is fired.

So is the producer. The executive in charge of the project takes it on herself to hire another writer. This one does a fine job but by the time he's finished the executive has also been fired and the woman who replaces her has her own agenda. Unfortunately that agenda does not include making my novel into a movie and it soon falls into that netherworld known as "turnaround," where the costs of another company acquiring the project are astronomical.

The option lapses.

My phone stops ringing. My book mysteriously disappears from the bookstores and a few weeks later I receive in the mail another rejection from the *New Yorker.* Because I'm depressed I run out and buy more drugs and alcohol. I invite my friends over to take my mind off things but half of them don't show up. They're lightweights. The party continues without them.

DEAL II

I am thirty-six years old and a little less confident. When an independent producer in New York options my third novel I am excited but cautious. In a year or two they might make the movie. Because it will be shot on a small budget, and because it will be only moderately successful, I can expect this novel to sell better than my last but by no stretch will it land on the best-seller list. I might appear on a local cable talk show. Maybe it will be a kind of cult hit. Above all the *New Yorker* will undoubtedly catch wind of this independent sleeper, recognize me for the undiscovered talent that I am, and publish one of my short stories. In the meantime the celebration begins. I run out and buy an eight-ball of methamphetamine because it is cheaper and stronger than coke, a few cases of Budweiser, a half-gallon of Smirnoff, Dewar's scotch and Seagram's 7 and invite my friends over for a party. But most of them are busy for some reason, and what few do show end up leaving early when I make an ass of myself. They're lightweights anyway.

This time the novel I sold is about an old man who runs a little theater out of a hotel in downtown Los Angeles, a hotel that's slated for demolition to make way for a freeway. He and his friend, a young alcoholic playwright, attempt to stage one last production before the building is razed, and time is running out. Of course there's more to it, a lot more, which is one of the problems in adapting it into a screenplay. But I'm willing to try.

The producer flies out from New York and we meet at Starbucks in Brentwood. He is an older, impeccably well-dressed gentleman, and he stands out in this crowd of mostly college students dressed in tank tops and flip-flops,

"You realize," he says, "that there'll have to be some changes."

"What kind of changes?"

"Don't worry," he says. "They're nothing major."

He takes a sip of his coffee. He sets it back down and dabs his mouth with his napkin. "For instance," he says, "I don't think the young playwright should be alcoholic. Alcoholics are detestable people and don't make for likable characters."

I wonder if he realizes that he is working with one. I wonder if he notices that my hands tend to shake around the time it is now, happy hour, a little after five o'clock. I need a drink but any suggestion I might've had of carrying this meeting over to the bar across the street is dashed.

The producer is an articulate, intelligent man, and during the course of our meeting he gives me several pages of notes, all of them insightful. I want to do a good job, and once more I'm willing to mercilessly cut and chop, create new scenes and eliminate others.

Inside of six months we have a strong screenplay with the original vision of the novel still intact. The producer shops it around to actors, directors and studio executives. A year passes. No luck. The call comes from Vermont, where he's vacationing, and I can sense by the tone of his voice that he's given up.

"You wrote a good script," he tells me. "But they're all saying it's too soft."

My phone stops ringing. My book mysteriously disappears

from the bookstores. I think it's all over and then out of the blue he phones again to tell me, in short, that I'm fired.

"What I think we need," he says, "is a fresh eye."

The new draft arrives in a manila envelope a couple of months later. The story, which originally took place in downtown Los Angeles, now opens in the jungles of Vietnam. But I'm not shocked. I'm not angry. I set the script aside after reading a few pages and reach for the other manila envelope that also arrived in the day's mail, the one with my own handwriting on it. It's from the *New Yorker*, and I'm hoping, as I split the envelope, that someone has been kind enough to include a word of encouragement on the rejection slip enclosed.

Because I'm depressed I invite my friends over for a party to help take my mind off things. But no one shows up. It's just as well. This way I don't have to share my dope and alcohol. I party alone with a gram of meth and a half-gallon of Popov's vodka.

DEAL III

I'm forty-three years old now and not so hopeful anymore. Maybe I am even a little bitter. When my fourth novel is optioned by another independent producer, this one from London, I am guarded. Before the year is up I'll deliver what I believe is a decent screenplay and then I'll be fired. Because the movie probably won't get made, and because my book probably won't sell any better than my others, I'll bank the money I make and be thankful I got it. In the meantime the celebration begins. I make reservations at a nice Mexican restaurant and invite my closest friends to dinner, the worst of the lightweights, the ones who prefer me clean and sober. We drink Martinelli's sparkling cider and espresso and have a great time.

This last novel is a coming-of-age story, a love story about a son and his father and an ex-prostitute with a passion for crime. They're on the run from the law, beginning on the banks of the Willamette River in Oregon and ending in catastrophe in Las Vegas. Of course it's more complicated than this, and capturing those complications in a script won't be easy, but I'm ready to try. I'm ready to give it my best shot.

The producer flies out from London and we meet at the Four Seasons in Beverly Hills. He's a pale Englishman and we conduct our meeting over lunch under a cabana at poolside. Like his New York counterpart, he is intelligent and articulate, though considerably younger. His first movie has just been released, one of the actors has been nominated for an Oscar, and it is doing well here and abroad. As we talk a young woman in a bikini strolls by our cabana, and I think I recognize her. I think I've seen her on TV but I don't remember where.

"It's a terrific novel," he says. "But I'm sure you understand we'll have to make some changes."

"What kind of changes?"

"Let's have a drink first," he says.

He orders vodka on the rocks. I order a seltzer water with a twist of lime. I like this man. He believes in my work, enough to invest his time and money, and it's my responsibility to do the best job I can. I also know that I'm not getting any younger and these opportunities won't continue to fall in my lap.

Once again, when I leave our meeting, I am prepared to mercilessly cut and chop. The difference this time around is that the producer has already interested an up-and-coming director in our project and soon I receive pages and pages of notes from both of them. I write a first draft.

They like it and want me to do another. They are already talking to studios, actors and finance companies. There is interest.

There is buzz.

I put in long hours on the next draft. I labor over every scene, every line of dialogue. In under a month I finish and send it off. The producer calls after he reads it and he's excited.

"I like it enormously," he says.

Those are his exact words, and I can still hear them, echoing in my head, when he phones a week later to fire me.

"The director," he says, "feels that it's uninspired. What I think we need on this is a fresh eye."

Before he can hire a new writer, however, the director hits

it with a big movie and wants nothing more to do with our project. The producer's interest wanes.

The option lapses.

My phone stops ringing. My book mysteriously disappears from the bookstores and soon another rejection slip from the *New Yorker* arrives in the mail. It sounds like the same old story but something has changed this time. Something about it feels brand-new. Maybe it has to do with that third strike. Maybe it's about the other close calls, too, the hopes they inspired and my coming to realize how few ever get the shots I've had. I'm sure of one thing, though. It's not about Hollywood anymore, or getting drunk and wasted, and in some ways it never has been. This is a bigger story now. One about change. Adaptation and acceptance. The drafts are endless but it's the writer, not the story, who undergoes the most important revisions.

A FINE PLACE

In the trunk we have four IBM self-correcting Selectrics, five adding machines and three Dictaphones. In the backseat, hidden under a blanket, are a Pioneer stereo, a half-dozen eight-track tape decks and a thirteen-inch Zenith color TV, brand-new, still in the box. I am fourteen years old. My friend Tito is sixteen, and we are unloading these items from his mother's Buick, items I helped him acquire. This takes place in an alley behind a used-furniture store in Watts, and I remember it vividly, this summer of 1970, because it is the first time I used heroin.

The woman buying these things works at the furniture store. She wears high heels and a tight dress made of shiny blue fabric. She's shaved off her eyebrows and penciled them in with black eyeliner, and I find this odd. I find it hard not to stare. She talks to Tito, not me, because they know each other from past dealings. He has sold her stolen goods before.

"You can keep the tape decks," she says. "I'll give you four hundred for the rest."

"Why not the decks?"

"I don't need them."

"Ten each," Tito says.

"Five," she says.

"Shit," he says. "The wiring is worth more than that."

On one side of the alley are the back entrances and loading docks for the different businesses that face Vermont Avenue. On the other side are the garages and carports of the run-down apartments and houses that face the neighboring street. The woman points to a bright yellow garage just across from the furniture store. "You boys can put the stuff in there," she says. "I'll walk you over." Tito reaches into the trunk for one of the Selectrics. I take another. It weighs about sixty, seventy pounds but feels light in my arms because the adrenaline is rushing and I am abnormally strong. What I want, and I want it badly, is to unload the car, collect our money and get out of here. Tito is experienced at this kind of thing and senses my anxiousness.

"Relax, Brown," he says. "You're sweating like a motherfucker."

Inside the garage are four or five black men standing around a workbench in the corner. A dim lightbulb dangles from an extension cord strung along the rafters and the smell of something burning hangs in the air. One of the men looks up at the woman and nods. The others glance at us, then turn away, and it makes me curious, what it is they're doing, how completely it consumes them. The man in the middle of the group is in the process of unfastening a belt from around his arm, and when we leave the garage, when we return with another load he is slumped in a chair, his eyes closed.

We set the stuff on the concrete floor, and on the way back to the car again I ask Tito about him, the man in the chair.

"What's wrong with that guy?"

"Nothing," he says.

"He looks wasted."

"Wasted good," Tito says. "Where he's at right now nobody, nothing, can touch him. It's a fine place, man, a beautiful place."

Later, when we've collected our money, Tito buys two bags of heroin for forty dollars and we drive back across town to the mountains of Griffith Park. At sixteen he has already fixed before. "A couple times," he tells me. "And it's a real trip." But I am fourteen, a virgin to the needle, and scared. I have heard the horror stories in school about drug addiction and junkies, stories designed to frighten, but still, or in spite of them, I want to go to that fine place where nothing can touch me. I see it as a kind of test, a kind of dare. With his teeth, Tito tears a strip from an old beach towel he found in the trunk of the car and ties it around my arm.

We are parked now along a quiet mountain road overlooking Hollywood, and in the distance, as Tito tightens the knot, I think I can see all the way to the Pacific. I don't want to watch what he's doing. I don't want to see the needle going in, and so I look out on the city spread before me. "Make a fist," Tito says. The sun is just setting, a thin layer of smog hangs in the sky, and the colors, refracted through the fading light, are remarkable. Pinks. Yellows. Shades of purple and brown. "Hold still," he says, and then I feel it, the sting, like a mosquito bite. The rush is deep, warm and profound. It's as if I'm sinking into myself, and for several moments, instead of feeling pleasure I am panicked, because I don't know where or how far it's taking me, how deep I'm going down. But then it levels out and I find myself somewhere between wakefulness and dream. Tito laughs, but his laughter sounds hollow, distant, like an echo.

In the summer of 1970, after a lengthy battle, my brother receives a psychiatric deferment from the United States Army. This is during the Vietnam War and he says he would kill himself if he were drafted. He says he would kill those who come to take him away in self-defense, fully expecting to go to prison or terminate his own life. In this memory I am troubled for my brother. In this memory I am sitting at the table in the kitchenette at his apartment and he is standing in the living room in front of the window that overlooks the rooftops of the shops and stores along Hollywood Boulevard.

We are drinking Wild Turkey 101 from styrofoam cups but it's too strong for me. I'm not keeping up.

"You don't really mean that stuff," I say, because I am concerned.

"About what?"

"Killing yourself."

He speaks casually, with false bravado, and it angers me.

"Maybe," he says. "Maybe not."

"Don't mess with me," I say. "You made it up to get out of the draft. That's all."

He laughs, and for a moment I relax and laugh with him. I like to believe that it's all just a smoke screen, an acting role, another stellar performance that commences years earlier, when he first sees a psychiatrist. He goes not because he wants help but because he needs to establish a psychiatric record for himself, knowing full well that whatever he tells the doctor will later appear on the report to the draft board. My brother is a fine actor and his plan works. I'm relieved that he won't be going to Vietnam but that doesn't stop me from worrying. His drinking is getting out of hand, though it has yet to take its toll in physical terms; at his age the body is remarkably resilient. Barry is strong and handsome, his career is going well, and for all outward appearances he is a model of success.

A copy of his psychiatric report rests on the table in front of me, and I read from it, silently, to myself: *An induction of this young man would result in personal catastrophe of either suicide or homicidal violence. In either condition he would be of no service or use in the Armed Forces.*

I push the paper aside.

"It's bullshit, right?"

"I don't know."

"What'd you mean you don't know?"

"It doesn't matter anymore, does it? I'm not being drafted."

I want to believe him, and I do. In this scene, at this moment, his rationalizations are enough for me. Free of the draft, there is no threat to his life or another's. But some years later, when I'm going through his belongings and come across the psychiatric report, I will know I believed a lie.

This takes place at a small Equity-waiver theater on La Cienega Boulevard in Hollywood. Again the year is 1970. Again it is summer, and my sister is performing tonight in an experimental play, an ensemble piece designed to showcase the talents of the various members of her acting class. The teacher is a veteran character actor who rarely works anymore, who survives now from the proceeds of his teaching, and he is staging this production for the benefit of his students. He is also the playwright and director. According to my sister there will be important agents, producers and directors in the audience tonight, and they will all be looking for new talent. Marilyn is both nervous and excited. She wants what Barry is now getting, recognition, but so far it has eluded her.

My memory of this night opens in the theater: my mother and I, sitting on hard wooden fold-out chairs, fanning ourselves with our programs, waiting for the play to begin. The place is packed, and with no windows, no fans or air-conditioning, it is uncomfortably warm, the air unpleasant to breathe. Still I'm looking forward to watching my sister perform and I am sure that our mother feels the same. My brother is conspicuously absent from this picture.

Because there are thirty students in Marilyn's acting class, and because the teacher wants to give each of them the opportunity to be seen, there are thirty roles in the play. This makes the story hard to follow with the different actors coming and going onstage and occasionally all of them appearing at once. I am confused much of the time but I attribute this confusion to my inexperience and lack of education. Certainly the play has hidden meanings, meanings that escape the simple mind of a fourteen-year-old boy, and because they escape me I am sure they must be significant and profound. Unfortunately Marilyn is just one of thirty hopefuls, and in the end, when the curtains are drawn, I feel that she's been cheated, the display of her talents shortchanged, lost in the chaos.

When she meets up with us outside the theater, her cheeks are flushed and she's smiling. She's also with one of the other actors, a man considerably older than her. He has long hair. He wears bell-bottom jeans and a tie-dyed T-shirt and I have the feeling that he's trying too hard to be hip. Our mother puts her arm around Marilyn and hugs her.

"You did good, honey," she says. "But how come you can't act in something like *Hello, Dolly!* Or *Bye Bye Birdie?* How come you let yourself get mixed up in these junky little plays? It was so hot in there Jimmy almost passed out."

"I did not," I say.

"You did, too."

"I see Barry didn't make it," my sister says.

Clearly she is disappointed. For her, Barry is already a highly accomplished actor, and she yearns for his approval, his attention. As a brother. As a teacher. But she rarely gets it anymore, not since he moved out, and sometimes it angers me— that he doesn't seem to care about her more.

"Mom," she says, "I want you to meet a friend of mine."

This friend will be the man Marilyn one day marries, and at first I don't like him any better than our mother does. For one thing, he's too old for her. For another, I know what he's after with my beautiful young sister, and I don't trust him. At the same time I can see that she's happy with him, and in Barry's absence I'm somehow relieved that he's here for her tonight. In light of his presence, however, our plans to take Marilyn to dinner are dashed, and the last thing I remember about this night is my sister climbing onto the back of her boyfriend's motorcycle. It's a classic image from a thousand movies: two lovers speeding down the boulevard and disappearing into the bright lights of the promised land.

It's around nine or ten at night and I am home alone. Marilyn is out with her boyfriend, the one she will eventually marry. My mother is also with a man tonight. After years of not dating, she has finally taken off her wedding ring, the ring she wore to ward off suitors, and allowed another into her life. I've only met him twice, when he came to the apartment for her, and he seems nice enough, well dressed in a suit and tie. Really I have no opinion of him one way or the other except to say that I don't begrudge my mother for dating, as children of divorced parents so often do.

As for Barry, of late he plays an even smaller role in my life. This is still the summer of 1970 but he has recently landed his first starring role in a movie and is gone now shooting in Kansas. He won't return for several months.

In some ways I prefer it like this. The privacy. The freedom that comes with being alone. I have my own key and most of the time I come and go as I please, do what I want when I want. But I also miss them, and lately, more than ever, I've come to miss my father. It is quiet in the apartment, and tonight, as I wander into my room, undress and climb into bed, I find myself thinking about him, wondering if he's alone at this moment, if he's asleep already or up watching TV.

Then my mind drifts to Tito and the things we stole. The eight-tracks come from cars parked around the neighborhood. The TV and stereo belong to someone who lives in a ground-floor apartment across the street. The big stuff—the Selectrics, the Dictaphones and the adding machines—come from an office building in North Hollywood. I think about the good part of stealing, the adrenaline rush, the fear of being caught and the exhilaration of getting away with it. And the money, all the easy money. But when I close my eyes I see the man who lives in that apartment coming home after a long day's work and finding his place ransacked. I picture the people who work in the office building in North Hollywood and the look on their faces when they discover the same scenario.

They are shocked.

They are disgusted and outraged. I bet they think that a couple of punk kids are responsible, the kind of kids who shoot dope in parked cars at Griffith Park, who might wind up in prison someday, deservedly, and they would be right.

In the living room I hear the familiar sounds of my mother returning home. The clatter of keys tossed on the coffee table. The fall of her pumps, first one then the other as she removes and drops them on the carpeted floor. My bedroom door creaks open and a moment later she is leaning over me. I smell her breath, the sour odor of alcohol.

"Jimmy," she says, "you asleep?"

But I say nothing. She kisses me lightly on the forehead. She arranges the blankets around my shoulders, and I wait until she steps back, turning to leave, before I call to her.

"Mom," I say.

"What is it, honey?"

Up until tonight the thought has never occurred to me. It has never even crossed my mind, and so it startles me, wherever it comes from, as I am sure that it startles my mother.

"I want to live with Dad," I say.

My mother sits on the edge of the bed and looks at me. "Are you sure?" she asks. "Is this what you really want?" And what I say next hurts, it hurts us both, that one word, that simple *yes.*

At night Los Angeles is a blanket of lights. From my seat, on this plane, I look down on the neatly sectioned streets and the endless procession of cars snaking along the different freeways. I can see the glowing orange ball of a 76 Union station. I can see the green playing field of a neighborhood park bathed in bright flood lamps. But over the ocean, as the plane continues to rise, the sky falls into darkness, and for a while I find myself staring at nothing. I have made a choice, and this choice, for me, is a kind of death. At fourteen I am shedding one life to embrace another.

Though confident with my decision, I am nonetheless worried and confused. My mother agrees that a boy my age should be with his father but tells me that if, by chance, it doesn't work out, she will welcome me back. Barry also supports my decision—by phone from Kansas. "Dad," he says, "needs you as much as you need him." The only dissenter is my sister, who thinks I am making a mistake. Our father, she tells me, is not the man I imagine him to be. He failed us once when he let our mother take us from him and he will fail again with me. Prepare for disappointment. She reminds me that he is likely still seeing our old baby-sitter, the woman she believes ruined our parents' marriage, and she accuses me of disloyalty and desertion. I am running away—from myself, she says— when I should be grateful for the ones who really love me, who have been there for me in the past.

I will miss my sister.

I will miss my mother and brother. But I am also lonely for my father and have been for some time. What I need, whether I'm aware of it or not at this age, and I believe I am, is a stronger sense of belonging, of *home*. Intuitively I know that my father can fill this need and I am drawn to him despite my sister's warnings.

The flight is a short one, just under an hour, and soon the lights of the city of San Jose appear outside the window. I am one of the first to unboard, and I spot him before he spots me. He is standing toward the back of the crowd, dressed in his work clothes, khaki pants and khaki shirt. On his face is the look of anxiousness, and when I approach he smiles, opening his arms to me.

In the summer of 1970 I learn to hang drywall, tape, sand and texture. I learn rough framing. I learn how to roof a house and pound a nail straight and true. Each day, until school begins in the fall, I work long hours with this man I call my father, a man who up until this time I know little about.

At home I am expected to pick up after myself, to help with the dishes, laundry and cleaning. If I go out, I'm expected back at a certain hour, and if I'm late, I am grounded. I like the discipline. I like knowing that someone cares, and though I continue to miss my brother, sister and mother, I feel I've made the right choice. On workdays we rise before the sun and he makes us a breakfast of eggs, hotcakes, bacon, sausage or ham. Then we climb into the truck and head to the lumberyard for material or go straight to the job. My father doesn't believe in

midmorning or late-afternoon breaks so we only stop for what
he calls supper and I call lunch. Either way we rest only long
enough to eat our sandwiches. He is a driven man. He has always been a driven man but now that drive is motivated at least
in part by the fear of time.

My father is a dreamer.

My father believes that if he just works hard enough he
will somehow dig himself out from under his bankruptcy and
reclaim the wealth and security he lost because of our mother.
But he is already at an age when most men retire and his possibilities are limited.

We live in a rented house on the east side, the poor side of
San Jose, and for the first month after I arrive, until we can afford another bed, I sleep with my father. At night he tells me
stories about when he was growing up in the backwoods of
Oregon and how he used to hunt for deer and fish for salmon.
He tells me about the years he worked for the Southern Pacific
Railroad and laid tracks through mountainous terrain that up
until then no white man had ever seen. He tells me about the
Cherokee, how he admired and respected their love of nature,
and he teaches me to count to ten in their language. This is all
before he moved to California. "I came for the work," he says.
"For greater opportunity. I met your mother, we fell in love
and raised a family. There were good years, many good years."

Now he dreams of returning to Oregon. He wants to get

money enough ahead to build a summer house for Barry, Marilyn and me on the Chetco River and bring us together again as a family if only for a few months out of the year. My father has a talent for detail, and as he describes the Chetco River, the salmon leaping out of the water, the sun glinting off their backs, as he describes the mountains of his youth and the beauty of a grazing deer, I am there with him. It is real to me. It is a fine place, and I live in his stories as I will someday live in my own.

At seventeen I will leave for college. A few years after I graduate he will die. Looking back, I see myself at fourteen in bed beside him. The room is still and dark. The kid who shoots heroin, robs and steals is getting drowsy, his father's voice slowly fading, and when I fall asleep and wake up thirty years later as a middle-aged man, I realize that this brief time I spent with my father has much to do with why I am still here and my brother and sister are not.

MIDAIR

On that warm night in July you lift yourself up to the rail of the overpass above the Los Angeles River. All you're wearing is a T-shirt and panties. In the distance you hear the cars moving along the Hollywood Freeway and beyond it you see the glow of the city lights. I want to believe that you can feel the coolness of the steel rail beneath your bare feet. I want to believe that as you fall you feel nothing more than the wind rushing up against your face. There is no pain. No impact. In my dreams you are suspended in midair.

You are forty-four years old the night you storm out of the house in the heat of another fight with your husband, the last fight you will ever have, and end your lifelong battle with alcohol and drugs. That it happens in July, the month our brother lost this same battle, is no coincidence. You have never been able to reconcile Barry's death, you see it as I do, as a kind of desertion, as betrayal, and your pain only deepens through the years. You have been to psychiatrists of every bent and persuasion. You have exhausted the long list of pharmaceuticals, checked yourself in and out of rehabs and halfway houses, and none of it has been of any lasting help. I know it is more complicated than this. I know there are other roots and causes for your illness and that the first symptoms came earlier, in childhood, but when I look back over your life I see Barry's death as the trigger for your destruction. You're only in your twenties at the time, you have a child and a husband, and your dream of becoming a successful actor is still very much alive. Then one morning soon after he's gone you tell me you are standing at the sink doing dishes and it sweeps over you, like a wave, this knowledge that nothing will ever be the same. At that moment something dies inside of you and you know that you will never get it back.

The night I drive in from San Jose for Barry's funeral you are high, as I am, we are both very high, and a few months later, when mourning is no longer an excuse for drowning your sorrows, you have already slipped across that line into addiction. Your husband follows. He is a plumbing contractor and makes enough to keep you both well enough supplied. Of course I am not far behind. In another year, when I graduate from college and return to Los Angeles, I will be in that dark place right alongside you. Your husband will give me a job digging ditch and running pipe, he is generous with his dope, and almost every day for the next several years I will be strung out and wired. At night I work on my novel while I drink to steady my nerves and then in the morning, after a few restless hours of sleep, the process begins all over again. Sometimes after work, instead of returning to my apartment, you and I hang out in your living room and get loaded. Behind the liquor and cocaine you talk freely where normally you are quiet and shy. You have never thought of yourself as pretty. You have never had confidence. Growing up our mother tells you that your nose is too big, that your breasts are too small, and for your sixteenth birthday she buys you a long blond wig to wear when you go out on auditions. "Maybe it will change your luck," she says. "I'm only trying to be helpful, honey." But when you're high the shyness disappears and you feel pretty, you feel smart. You like to talk about actors. You like to talk about the movies you've seen or the books you've just read or the play you plan to audition for at that little theater on Lankershim, the ninety-nine-seater. I encourage you, try to build you up.

"Go for it," I say. "I know how good you are. I've seen you act."

Compliments make you uneasy, and when you smile, when you give a nervous laugh, you cover your mouth with your hand because you are self-conscious.

As proof of your talent I remind you about your close call for a role in a Woody Allen movie and how he found your shyness charming and took you for a walk around the block to help put you at ease before you read for the part. And you did well. You said so yourself and you are anything but a braggart. I don't mention that this close call was years ago or that you haven't auditioned for anything since. The longer you are out of the loop, the harder it is for you to regain the courage to get back in, and I worry that you have given up. You live in our brother's shadow but you have your own dreams and I know that if you let them slip away you will be bitter with regret for the rest of your life. So we have another drink. We do another line. What we share, you and I, is a sadness for our brother and this constant need, this craving to somehow make ourselves feel better.

The odds are against you and have been for some time. At nineteen you marry the first man who shows you love, that one who rides the motorcycle. He is fifteen years older than you and you tell me you marry him because he is a tradesman and reminds you of our father. That you like his rough hands. But the real reason is to escape from our mother and begin a new life. That you are already two months along only makes the decision easier, and over the weekend you fly out to Reno, to one of those gaudy chapels along the strip. Afterward you get drunk on champagne and they kick you out of Harrah's for gambling because you're underage and you laugh it off, you get drunker, and by Monday you're back in L.A. with your husband just in time for him to go to work.

For a while you are happy in your new role as housewife, as mother-to-be, and you spend your days getting the room fixed up for the baby. You hang wallpaper with bright rainbows and big white clouds. You take down the old blinds and replace them with curtains that let in more light. You shop for cute outfits, jumpers, bottles, diapers, and a mobile of stars and moons to hang over the crib that you've already put on layaway at Sears. These are good times. They fill you with a sense of pride and satisfaction in a way you've never known before. Then the baby arrives. It isn't as easy as you thought and you don't get out much anymore. Movies and restaurants seem a thing in the past. You want to be the best mother you can, and you try, you really do, but when the newness of it all wears off you start feeling frustrated again. Where you were once quick to answer your baby's call, now you sometimes shut the door and let her cry herself to sleep. Soon your house, like your life, seems smaller, and you feel as if you're caged in. There are moments when your heart races for no apparent reason and you can't quite catch your breath. Your doctor says it's just a typical reaction to the stresses of motherhood and prescribes Valium. He tells you that you need rest.

A drink in the late afternoon takes the edge off your hectic day, and when you mix it with the Valium it works even better. So long as you keep it to one or two, and no more than a bottle of chardonnay at dinner, you don't see the harm. God knows it's not easy caring for a colicky baby, and of course you love her, that's not the issue. It's just that sometimes you feel overwhelmed and it creeps up on you, especially late at night when the house is quiet and you're stretched out in bed with your eyes wide open, staring into the darkness and wondering if this is what it's all about, if this is all there is. As your husband lies beside you snoring it comes over you again, this vague sense that something is wrong, something is missing and maybe, just maybe, you married the wrong man. These feelings scare you and you want them out of your head, you want them gone *now.* A nightcap will help, just a shot or two of vodka in a little warm milk. That and another Valium always does the trick.

But when you wander down the hall to the bathroom and open the medicine cabinet you find that the bottle is empty. You can't believe it. You don't understand. Just last week it was close to full. You're certain of it because you remember explicitly how the pharmacist cautions you about refilling it early again and has to call your doctor. He puts you out. He makes you wait and it's all for nothing, since you end up getting exactly what you came for anyway. You give him a curt smile as you pay, and you pay quickly so he won't notice the trembling in your hands. In your car you take double the dose and swallow them dry. The taste is acrid and bitter and nearly makes you gag. You remember that part too well.

On your way back to bed that night it occurs to you that for some crazy reason maybe your husband hid your pills. You can't fathom why but just the possibility of it, the very idea that he might think you have some kind of problem infuriates you. This is your medication. This is *doctor* prescribed. You shake him awake. You ask him point-blank what he did with your Valium and he pretends like he doesn't know what you're talking about. It's not so much what he says as that sleepy dumb look on his face, that bullshit innocent look that makes you even angrier, and for what happens next you have no explanation. Something just snaps. You don't know what it is, or where it comes from, but suddenly you're out of control, screaming and pounding on him with your fists.

Tonight he doesn't strike back but eventually, as your addiction grows, as you continue to rage, he, too, will lose control. You will both fight. You will both hurt each other. I am living in San Francisco, going to college, when you phone in the middle of the night in tears.

"I've had it," you say. "It's over. I'm leaving the son of a bitch . . ."

In midsentence he yanks the phone from your hand and all I hear is your screaming. A moment later he's on the line.

"Jimmy," he says.

"What the hell's going on?"

"I'm really sorry but it's crazy around here. She'll have to call you back."

From some other part of the house I hear your child crying, and before the line goes dead there is another sound, the thud of a hard blow, your fist landing solid in the hollow of his back. All night long I try to get ahold of you but the line is off the hook. It's not until late the next afternoon when it finally rings, and when you pick it up your voice is cheerful. You even laugh.

"I guess I owe you an apology. We were drinking last night and things just got a little out of hand. You know how it is. You remember Mom and Dad."

"But he never hit her," I say. "It never was that bad."

You give me a heavy sigh like you think you know something that I couldn't possibly understand.

"Married people fight. That's just how it is. Don't make a big deal out of it. We're all right," you say. "I mean it, really, everything's fine."

At the time I judge you. I think you're lying to yourself and that your problems go far deeper than you're willing to admit. How, I wonder, can you be so blind? But my drinking and drugging will one day take me down the same path in my own marriage, and I will fight with my wife. I'll explode for no reason and phone you late at night, drunk and wired, while my children cry in the background. These memories hurt, and I have others, many far worse. They accumulate over the years and instead of fading with time they only grow more vivid. The shame and remorse builds. The load grows heavier as we age and I understand now how every day you find yourself a little closer to that overpass above the Los Angeles River.

After Barry dies the vodka and Valium are no longer enough. The cocaine works for a while, makes you pretty and smart, but where a few lines once took you to a better place now it requires much more. Between you and your husband the supply often runs out and soon he's pulling money from his contracting business, charging up the credit cards to cover the difference, bouncing checks and borrowing from friends. Staying high is a full-time job and you begin to let the small things slide. The beds don't get made. The dishes aren't washed. The laundry piles up and there's no point in vacuuming when you have a little brat who can't remember to wipe her feet no matter how many times you tell her.

What is she now? Four, five? I lose track of time. But she's growing up fast, and occasionally it strikes you, how you're missing out on some special years, how you can't ever get them back. Half the day you keep her in preschool and as soon as she gets home she locks herself in her room and stays there, watching TV, afraid to come out, afraid of what mood she might find you in. Sometimes you feel as if you hardly know her, your own daughter, and it pulls at your heart. You try to go without the drugs and booze for a couple of days and make plans to do something together. Go to a movie. Have a picnic at the park. Your intentions are good but somehow things just never seem to turn out right. The traits you see in your daughter are the same ones you see in yourself and have never liked. Her shyness. Her constant fidgeting and nail biting. The worst is how she always walks with her head down as if she has no pride, no confidence in herself. Part of you sympathizes with her while the other part, the sick part, condemns. You are already a person with little patience, but without the drugs and alcohol you're far worse. Inside of twenty-four hours you're depressed and tired and beginning to feel nauseous. Your moods swing from one extreme to the other. One moment you are raging at her for spilling her milk, and the next you are cooing in her ear, promising to read her a book. That fear you see in your daughter's eyes is a fear you know well. Later you're sick with remorse and you have a realization, one that's visited you before, and that is that you are a better person and a better mother when you're stoned out of your mind. For your sake and that of your child you have to feed the demons or they will destroy what is left of the goodness in your heart. I understand how you feel because I have done similar harm to my sons.

Going straight, even for a couple of days, isn't and can never be a viable option. You are convinced of this. You are resigned. If you need more evidence just remember the time that your dealer got busted and it took your husband two long agonizing weeks to hook up with another. Meanwhile you're crawling out of your skin, jonesing bad and drinking more than ever to kill the pain. You have to do something so you pay a visit to one of your old friends from high school, though he's not actually a friend, in fact you've never liked him, he's a seedy motherfucker but he's a seedy motherfucker with dope. The trouble is, you don't have enough money, and there you are again, doing something that you promised yourself you never would.

The shame and guilt eat at you until one night you can't take it any longer and you get so drunk it just spills out. Even as it's happening, before the words escape from your mouth, you know that you are making a terrible mistake. You tell me that you confess out of respect for your husband but you know that it's really about saving yourself. Add this to your list of best worst memories. It's another that only gets heavier through the years. I know this from my own experience. Though I'm not foolish enough to confess, my wife senses my infidelities well enough, and trying to carry on as if nothing has happened, as if I could ever reclaim her trust, is just another act of deception. But we are drunks. We are addicts and we behave recklessly without regard for the consequences of our actions. Sometimes slowly, sometimes quickly, we destroy the ones we love as surely as we destroy ourselves.

The years slip by. I quit your husband and the plumbing trade and return to school. I know you don't begrudge me for attempting to make a better life for myself but you also can't help seeing my leaving in the same light as you do Barry's suicide. You see it as a form of desertion, a kind of betrayal reminiscent of the first time I left you, years before, to live with our father. You feel I've used you and your husband and taken advantage of your generosity with drugs and that the only reason I ever came around was to get high.

You couldn't be more wrong.

What is true is that I care about my writing, as you once cared about your acting, and I had to make a break or my dream, like yours, would fade away. So I make that break and marry my first real love, as you married yours. Heidi and I met back in high school and she is good for me, she gives me strength, love and purpose, and for this I will always be indebted. Although she knows going into our marriage that I drink and use she believes that it will pass in time, that I'll grow out of it. In the early years she even does some experimenting herself, but drinking makes her feel out of control and cocaine just puts her on edge. "What's the point?" she says. "I wouldn't exactly call it fun, being wired or slurring my words." So she quits, except for an occasional drink or hit of marijuana, and this is why our marriage probably lasts as long as it does. Imagine if Heidi and I both used, how far we would've made it.

For a while I comport myself well enough. I keep my drinking and drugging to a minimum, and in trying to make a better life for us I enroll in graduate school at U.C. Irvine and continue work on my first novel, a novel that eventually gets published, gets optioned for a movie, sells paperback rights and sets us on our way. Meanwhile Heidi and I have our first child and I am there for her in the delivery room, stone-cold sober, holding her hand and giving whatever support a husband can give his wife when he is powerless to ease her pain.

I've never liked children.

They annoy me. They're loud and often obnoxious. They cry and make too many demands and I've never had the patience for them. But when Andy comes into the world I love him immediately in a way I never before knew I was capable of loving. He is a quiet, easy baby with few demands, and when Heidi returns to work as a display artist, while I'm completing my last year of graduate school, I take our son to classes with me. I carry him in a pouch that straps around my shoulders and rests on my stomach. I feed him. I change him. I love and comfort him.

I have not always been a bad father.

Later I will become a professor of English and jump from job to job—Irvine, Santa Clara University, Hayward State—until I settle, back in Southern California again, in the desert wastelands of San Bernardino. In that time my wife and I have had our second child, and this one is harder on us. He is colicky. He is hypersensitive to light and noise and prone to ear infections. His needs put an additional strain on our marriage, and I am strangely proud of myself, for despite my growing addictions I am for the most part there for the boy when his mother has reached her limits. Somewhere in through here I also publish a second novel, this one about the family, mainly Barry, and I fail to include you, my sister.

"Where am I?" you ask me, after you've read it. "Don't I matter? I lived this story with you. I mean, Christ, I was *there*."

Now that I'm older I realize the magnitude of my mistake. I realize that you are right. I do you and the novel a serious injustice by not sticking closer to the truth and the story ultimately suffers because of it. But at the time, in my selfishness, I tell you that you don't understand the constraints of the novel, what can and can't be included, and if you just look more closely you'll see how I leave out all sorts of things, all sorts of people, and it's not because these things didn't happen or that these people don't exist. It's because they don't fit. Don't belong. After all it is just fiction. After all it is about making things up, and you know it is easier to lie about the dead than the living.

By now your daughter is all grown up. She is your age when you gave birth to her and despite her childhood, or maybe because of it, she turns out to be a fine, responsible young woman who's seen what drugs and alcohol did to you and her father and won't touch them herself. You're in your late thirties now and still going strong. You've racked up three DUIs. You've wrecked two cars. Your husband has filed for bankruptcy but the coke is still plentiful, and your marriage, like mine, continues to erode. But there is hope. People change. Addicts and alcoholics can get better instead of sicker and I've seen it in you. You break the news to me over the phone.

"Are you sitting down?" you say. "Because you won't believe this. I don't believe it myself but I'm pregnant again."

Maybe neither of us voice it but we both know that this is your chance to turn your life and marriage around. This is the motivation you need to quit drinking and doping, and for the most part you do. In the months to follow you cut back to just a couple of drinks a day, and in the evening, to quell the withdrawal symptoms, you only take one Valium or Xanax instead of your usual three or four. And so far as the coke goes, because you've heard all those terrible things about crack babies, you use it only on the weekends and in moderation. Those who know little about addiction might see it as a moral weakness and expect nothing less from you than complete sobriety. But for someone who has drunk and used so much for so long I know that any step forward is a tremendous one and I am proud of you. At least you acknowledge your problem. At least the desire and effort to change is there, and even if it is not yet enough, you deserve a certain respect.

Your daughter is off at college, her room is empty, and again you begin making preparations. Because you never expected to have another child, you gave away the crib. You gave away the bassinet, threw out the old clothes and broken toys, and now you rise early in the morning, with a renewed sense of purpose, and look for replacements at garage sales and swap meets. You scour the papers for good deals. Hunt for bargains at department stores. You are eager to fill that room back up but mostly you are eager to fill yourself up again, and the baby offers you this chance, the promise of a new start. Things will be different this time. You will be a responsible mother, you will do the job right, make amends with the past and free yourself of your guilt and shame. The old wounds of your marriage will heal and you and your husband will fall in love all over again, only this time it will be a stronger, more mature love because you have had to overcome so many obstacles to finally get there. In some ways you see this baby as your last hope for a so-called normal, happy life, and it takes you back to earlier days when you were a churchgoer, a firm believer in God.

"I know you're not religious," you say, "and I'm not big on it either anymore. But I really believe this is my wake-up call. I really believe this baby is a gift from God."

Since you are no longer a young woman, you have an amniocentesis done. You take a sonogram. The doctor tells you that everything is fine, the baby is perfectly healthy. Is it a boy? you ask. A girl? Where with your first you wanted to be surprised, this time you want to know up front so that you can be better prepared, if only for the baby shower. You say it's the practical thing to do but I have a feeling that you're just too excited to wait, and I like that about you. It's part of your charm. You and your husband name her Katherine and paint her room a light shade of pink.

When your water breaks and the contractions start, your husband drives you to the hospital. You don't have medical insurance so the care isn't what it should be and they hook you up to a fetal monitor and leave you in the room alone. The intervals between contractions grow closer together and more intense. You're nervous. You're scared. You feel the baby moving inside you and know the time is near. But where is your husband? He should be here holding your hand and dabbing your forehead with cool, damp washcloths. He calls me late at night, shortly after you're admitted. I worked with this man for several years and I suspect, by the way he speaks, that he is high.

"Congratulations," he says. "You're about to be an uncle again."

"How's she holding up?"

"She was doing fine when I left."

"What'd you mean? Where are you?"

"At home," he says. "I couldn't find a parking space and I had to run back and get some money. I forgot my wallet."

It doesn't make sense. You double-park, you take a ticket or let your car be towed, but you don't leave your wife alone in the hospital when she's having your baby. Did he really need the money? Or did he really go home for more dope? Either way he now has to live with this. While you are alone in that strange room in that hospital, the fetal monitor makes an odd noise but at first you think nothing of it and there's no one around, no doctors or nurses, not even your husband to tell you differ-ent. Still, to be on the safe side, you press the button on the rail of the bed. A minute passes. No one comes. You press it again and then you feel something or maybe it's that you don't feel anything at all. The baby is floating motionless inside you with the umbilical cord wrapped around her neck.

Maybe if your husband had been there he could've gone for help. Maybe because you don't have any insurance the nurses don't respond as quickly. This is a busy hospital that serves more than its share of the poor and they'll get to you when they can. The Christian God is a punishing god and hereafter you will believe that He has taken your child in payment for your sins as a drug addict and alcoholic. The guilt and shame weigh heavy on you but the loss of baby Katherine is in one way still a gift: For the next four years you and your husband remain clean and sober.

He quits cold turkey. You check yourself into rehab. You join A.A. and replace the compulsion to drink and use with the compulsion to attend meetings twice a day, seven days a week, and they add up to possibly the best years of your life. Somehow you rebuild your relationship with your daughter. Somehow you and your husband are able to put the past behind you and love one another in ways you were both never before capable. You are a different person, even-tempered and calm, and now you assume a role in my children's lives. You read them bedtime stories when they spend the night. You throw them birthday parties and take them to movies and surprise them with goblin and ghost costumes for Halloween and insist that we visit every Fourth of July to light fireworks in your driveway.

"It's like the old days," you tell me. "It's like when we were kids and could still enjoy life without having to get loaded."

I hardly remember those times myself, since I was even younger than you when we first started drinking and using, and I have only a vague sense of what you mean. Dope and alcohol are still my good friends and I'm not yet willing to let them go. While you are busy staying sober, I am busy getting high. I have graduated from cocaine to methamphetamine. Where a gram of coke might last you a day, the same amount of this dope wires you for a week, and it's taking me down fast. I have to drink more in order to sleep at night, if I sleep at all, and in the morning I have to double up on the meth to offset the hangover. I wake up mean. I wake up angry at myself and the world and my moods swing from one extreme to another as yours once did. I belittle my wife. I ignore my children. One moment I am raging, the next I'm apologizing for saying or doing something I should never have said or done.

Then there is the other side that surfaces from time to time, the better side when I'm in control of myself and my moods and I take my family out to see a movie or involve the boys in soccer, Little League and wrestling. I *can* be good even in the midst of my addiction. I *can* be responsible. It's within me and always has been. Remember, too, that I work hard. That I'm under considerable pressure and we all get moody now and then. So long as I have a good job, I reason, and money enough left over after the bills to buy my liquor and drugs everything is fine. After all I'm still writing. I'm still publishing, and in my five-year teaching evaluation the chair of my department refers to me as an "outstanding citizen with a record of excellence in and out of the classroom."

And I actually believe it.

I'm the first to admit that I occasionally drink a little too much, and I know I should quit the speed, or at least cut back, but it's not as if I have a problem. This is why after a three-day bender, and my wife and I have another big fight, I let you talk me into going to an A.A. meeting. I do it to appease my wife and children. I do it to appease you. The meeting is held in a church in North Hollywood and the place is packed. People I've never seen before greet you as if they are your dearest friends. You hug them. You smile. It's too much for me, these public displays of camaraderie and affection, and the meeting itself strikes me as nothing less than a mass confession.

One after another pours his heart out to the group. I am stunned that anyone in good conscience could bare their feelings in front of so many strangers, and I see them as weaklings. As whiners. The religious overtones, the constant references to God and a Higher Power, put me off. Everything is a "miracle" to these people, from finding a parking space to lasting another day without a drink, and after a while all their stories begin to sound the same. They have lost wives and husbands because of their drinking. They have lost jobs, been jailed and institutionalized. They are housewives and dentists. They are lawyers and hairdressers, carpenters and waiters, clerks and actors and nurses strung out on Vicodin.

If I learn one thing that afternoon it's that there are a whole lot of others out there more messed up than me and knowing this somehow makes me feel better about myself. I've never wrecked a car. I've never been busted. I've never lost a job. All this goes to show is that I don't have a real problem with alcohol or drugs. In the car, on the way back to your house, I tell you these things and you laugh.

"Those are what they call the 'yets' and it just means you're lucky. So far anyway. Trust me, they'll happen if you keep drinking." You laugh again. "Never underestimate the power of denial."

I don't like the tone of your voice. I don't like how you laugh. You think you know something about me that I don't and I resent you for it. I am offended because your words are true and I'm not ready to hear them yet. In time I will, but not now. You're a convert in what I see as a cult and I know better than to argue. What concerns me is you. And I don't care what it takes. If believing in God gives you hope, if confessing to others helps you through another day, then you need to stick with it. It may not be right for me but it's clearly working for you and that's all that matters.

Tell me, then.

What happened?

Why after four years of being clean and sober do you get up out of your seat in the middle of the movie that night and say to your husband that you have to use the bathroom and instead leave the theater and walk across the street to the liquor store? I know the rationalizations. I know my own typical excuses. This time, you think, it will be different. This time you'll be able to control it. Four years without a drink or a drug proves only one thing—that you're all better now, absolutely *cured*. You consider it a test, one you're certain to pass, and because you're so certain, you see no harm in opening the bottle and raising it to your lips. You only plan to take one drink and then hurry back to the theater. But one doesn't prove anything. You need a second. You need a third and after that, in a matter of minutes, you're not thinking about your husband sitting by himself in the theater waiting for you, wondering where you've gone.

There's a park nearby. It has some picnic tables where you can relax and drink under the cover of darkness. The night is cool and you wish you had brought your sweater but you have the vodka to warm you, so you drink a little faster. You are not there long when a man approaches. The alcohol has clouded your judgment and you have no fear. You offer him a drink. For a while you just talk and pass the bottle back and forth, but when you get up to leave you find out that he wants something more, and he takes it. The police pick you up the next morning wandering naked through the park, and later you tell me that you don't remember a thing after he dragged you into the bushes. That's when you blacked out, and this is good, because this is another memory that only brings you closer to that overpass above the L.A. River. Your husband calls me from the hospital.

"Marilyn was raped last night."

"Oh God."

Silence.

"Is she all right?"

"How can she be all right after something like this?" he says. "If you mean did he beat her up, no. She's not hurt that way."

"I want to see her."

"I don't think that's a good idea."

"What're you talking about," I say. "She's my sister, man."

"She got drunk again. That's how it happened. She got drunk again and ended up in the park. I don't want her around drunks and you're a drunk, Jimmy, you're a fucking drunk. Don't call her. Don't come around. You're not welcome in our house anymore."

He hangs up.

Ever since baby Katherine's death I have blamed your husband for failing you, for feeding your addictions, and now he is turning my logic against me. We are both guilty. We are both somehow responsible but I'm not ready yet to accept my part. All I feel for your husband is anger. He is keeping me from seeing you, he is suddenly self-righteous about his sobriety, and I resent him for judging me even if what he says is true. If I were any kind of brother I would not have let him drive this wedge between us, but I am deep into my own sickness, deeper than I ever imagined possible, and I am of no use to you or anyone in my life. This is how I rationalize it, anyway, why I'm not there for you, why I barely try.

For all intents and purposes my marriage is over. I still love her, she is a good woman, but the damage we've done to each other over the years is irreparable, and now I often find myself sleeping at a friend's apartment or passing out in my car along some deserted mountain road. Anything but come home to another fight. I don't know how I keep my job. The days just bleed one into another in an alcohol and drug-induced haze. That period of my life is blurred, the memories fractured, incomplete. But somehow in this haze I meet another woman, the woman who will later become my second wife, and if there was ever the slightest chance of rebuilding my marriage it is lost now. The divorce is long. The divorce is bitter, and my children, close friends, relatives and in-laws, everyone seems to take sides. My oldest son has seen me hurt his mother too often and chooses to stay with her. Nate, he's only three when we divorce and has no voice in the matter. Our middle boy wants to live with me but Heidi files an emergency order with the court stating that because of my alcohol and drug abuse I am an unfit father. If I don't agree to all her terms and conditions, she threatens to take the children away from me permanently. There will be no shared custody. No visiting rights. "You'll never see the boys again," she says. Even you, my sis-

ter, condemn me for a deserter, a failed husband, a failed father. This is another reason why we lose contact near the end
of your life.

The last time I see you is at a place called the Friendly
House on Normandie Avenue on the outskirts of downtown
Los Angeles. It is a live-in recovery home and you are there
because once you started drinking again you've been unable
to stop. You've gotten another DUI. You've passed out in
your bathroom and split open your head on the hard porcelain sink. Your husband has come home from work and
found you in the kitchen, facedown in your own vomit, and
another time in the hallway soaked in urine. Your alcoholism
has advanced to its final stages, and sobriety is now a simple
matter of life and death. But when I visit you at the recovery house you are several months sober, and I have nine days
behind me, more consecutive clean time than I've had since I
was twelve. You look good. I'm still shaky. We sit in the
kitchen and drink coffee, a far cry from the earlier days of
vodka and cocaine.

"Those first thirty days are a bitch," you tell me. "But the
bloat's going away and your eyes are clear. You should be proud
of yourself, Jimmy. I am."

I hand you a small jewelry box and you open it up. Inside
is a gold cross on a thin gold chain. You smile.

"I haven't had one of these since I was a little girl," you say, as you unfasten the clasp and slip it around your neck. "Don't tell me you're getting religious in your old age."

"No," I say, "I just thought you'd like it."

"I do."

"It's made in Italy."

I don't know why I mention this. I guess it's supposed to matter since we are half Sicilian from our mother's side but they just hang there, those words, empty of meaning.

Long visits are not encouraged. You have a strict daily schedule of meetings, counseling and chores, and we part on a good note, hugging each other, wanting to believe that we will both be all right. And for the moment that possibility seems real and true. That we *can* change. Yet inside we are scared because we know this hope is fleeting and that the better life we imagine for ourselves may just be another illusion. The bottle, pills and powders own us and we are fooling ourselves if we think we can survive without them. I make it something like twelve days. You last four months and then, because you're doing so well, the counselors let you go home for the weekend to be with your husband. But on Monday morning, when you're supposed to return to the recovery house, you're too drunk to get out of bed. Your husband is disgusted. Your counselors have had it and won't take you back.

So you're on your own now. For a while you double up on your A.A. meetings, call your sponsor five or six times a day and work the twelve steps religiously. But it's the same old story, you get a day or two sober and then go out again, each binge worse than the last, and eventually, inevitably, you alienate all the people who love and care about you. You have drained all your resources. You have cut all ties. Ruined all relationships. You are now among the living dead who for whatever reasons cannot or will not stop drinking.

This is when your late-night calls begin again, while I'm still going through my bitter divorce, struggling to stay sober and living with the woman who helps me toward this end, the woman I will later marry. I've put together three months at this point, and like the others in your life I have run out of patience. Each time you phone you are drunk, full of anger and self-loathing, and you direct it at me because it is eating you up inside. Your husband doesn't understand you. He never has. You cry over the death of baby Katherine and blame me and yourself for Barry's suicide. Mom is a petty criminal. Dad is a dumb redneck. You cry over our rotten childhood and tell me you were never loved, never felt love, that it was all a big lie. The rape, you never talk about.

Sometimes I let you carry on. Sometimes I just have to hang up. All the calls are the same except for one, the last, and you're sober. But when I answer the phone that morning and hear your voice again I immediately assume the worst.

"What do you want?" I say.

"I just called to talk."

"I'm busy."

"Doing what?"

"It doesn't matter. I don't have time to fight right now."

"I don't want to fight, either," you say.

But I don't believe you.

"I have to go," I say.

"Jimmy," you say. "Don't hang up. Please don't hang up."

There's a long silence. I twist the cord of the receiver around my hand.

"What," I say. "What do you want?"

"I want to apologize."

"For what?"

"These last few months. I know I've been acting crazy and taking it out on you and everybody else and I want to tell you I'm sorry."

"It's okay," I say. "I'm not any better when I drink."

"No, it's not okay. I need to know if you still love me."

"Of course I do."

"I love you, too. You know I do, no matter how I act, no matter what I say."

Another silence passes.

"Can I ask a favor?"

"Maybe," I say, because I'm still skittish. I'm still on guard.

"Do you mind if your kids spend this weekend with me? I

know it's your time with them but I'd really like to see them again. It's been a while."

"Sure," I say, and when we hang up I feel better about myself and you.

What I do not realize is that this is your way of saying good-bye to them and me. I understand that last weekend with my boys went well, you took them to a carnival near your house, everyone had a good time, and I respect you for this final gesture. I love you all the more for it. But on Sunday, after their mother picks them up, you drink again and begin to rage. Your husband takes the bottle away and empties it into the sink. He hides the car keys. He confiscates your purse, your money and credit cards, and then locks himself in the bedroom. You pound on the door. You scream but he just turns up the TV and you storm out of the house in the heat of another fight.

This is July, the month our brother killed himself, and the night is warm. All you're wearing is a T-shirt and panties. The overpass on Lankershim Avenue is just around the block, and soon you are there, lifting yourself up to the rail. The Los Angeles River is no river at all but a narrow concrete channel that runs thirty, maybe forty feet below. In the distance you hear the cars moving along the Hollywood Freeway and beyond it you can see the glow of the city lights. The steel rail is cool beneath your bare feet and you feel a warm summer breeze pass along your face. Do you think of baby Katherine? Can you picture your husband and daughter? Do you see me, your brother?

Because I am standing beside you.

The following morning a passerby spots your body and phones the LAPD and soon the patrol cars are on the scene. A police helicopter hovers overhead. The noise and commotion bring your husband out of the house, and because he's been looking for you, because you've been missing for thirteen hours, he hurries to where the crowd has gathered. I find out that same night, from Heidi, who despite our bitter divorce takes me into her arms as she delivers the news: Your sister killed herself. She's gone. I'm so sorry.

Later, when your ashes are scattered at sea, I learn from your husband that you had talked about taking your life for some time. Had I known, would it have mattered? Could I have made the difference? Marilyn, you know I would've tried.

In the beginning the alcohol and drugs bring you relief. They give you courage and confidence and then, slowly, over a period of years, they strip it all away and you spend your final years struggling to fill the emptiness that it's left inside you. It's futile, it's madness, and for you and our brother there is only one way to end the pain. This is the choice you make. I have no right to judge what you are capable of enduring. But in my dreams I am standing beside you on that rail of the overpass above the L.A. River, and I reach for your hand. You look at me and smile.

"Don't worry," you say. "There's nothing to be afraid of anymore."

Then you squeeze my hand and let go and I watch you fall, again and again, as I will for the rest of my life. There is no more pain. No impact. In my dreams you are suspended in midair, the wind rushing up around you, captured in the moment of flight.

SOUTH DAKOTA

First I feel chilled. Then come the cold sweats and this tin-gling sensation up and down my arms like ants are crawling just beneath the surface of my skin. Except for that part the symptoms resemble the flu. I run a slight fever, too, and there is definitely nausea. But I keep right on talking, a real trouper. I don't miss a beat.

If I seem fatigued, or disoriented at moments, it's only be-cause I flew in a couple of nights before. This explains the bloodshot eyes and the dark circles. As for that gaunt look, everybody knows skinny is fashionable in California. These are the things I want the students to believe but the truth of the matter is much different. I am a visiting writer-in-residence at the University of South Dakota, on leave from my permanent job at Cal State San Bernardino, and this is the first session of the first week of class. The month is March, and outside it is cold. Outside a thin layer of frost and snow covers the school grounds but inside this building, in this classroom, it is stifling hot.

I take off my sweater. Underneath I'm wearing a V-neck T-shirt, an old one, thinning, not long for the rag pile. But right now it's hard to care about how I'm dressed. The sweating hasn't stopped and the nausea isn't going away, either. It comes in waves and the intervals between visits seem to be getting shorter. At some point I get around to the student story that we're supposed to be discussing.

I know I read it carefully on the plane. The chair of the English department mailed it to me before I left San Bernardino, at my request, this story as well as several others, so that I would be prepared for the first week. No downtime. That's the way I like it. They are paying me well and I believe that the students deserve their money's worth. Then, an hour before class, I read it again. Ask me what it's about now, though, and the best I could manage is a sketchy description of its main character, a young thief. I don't mean this as a comment on the quality of the story, that I can't remember it.

The fact of the matter is, I read a lot of stories. It's what I do for a living, that and try to write them myself, and after a while I just forget, even the best ones. And my own, too, I especially forget my own. In this case, though, it is not a good story, because the writer doesn't know much about thieves and is bent on sermonizing. I remember feeling that as plainly as the tingling sensation under my skin, those ants, and trying not to scratch at them.

The writer, a Ph.D. candidate in American literature, isn't thinking like a thief. He's looking at the character from too far away, a good distance for judging maybe but not intimacy, not understanding. I like to let the students have their say first so that my point of view doesn't unduly influence their own, and after we've gone around the room, when everyone has had a chance to comment on the story, I raise my own concerns. I am careful with my words. I am conscious of how my criticism might affect the writer, and so I choose the gentler road, up and around the subject, even if it takes a little longer to get the point across. I want to be helpful. I want to be liked. There are ways, I believe, to express yourself without unnecessarily offending the writer.

When I'm done, a student raises her hand. She is a bright woman who later proves to be one of the more talented writers in class, and she's upset.

"Let me get this straight," she says. "According to you, we're supposed to *like* this lowlife? All he does is go around ripping people off. I don't see why we have to sympathize with him."

Sympathy isn't the right word, and I don't recall using it. It's understood that stealing is wrong. Thieves know it, too. That it hurts people, even themselves. What I want to know is that they might otherwise live respectable lives, or at least that this thief does. Make him a family man, a loving husband at one time. Give him a couple of kids and show him coaching Little League on the weekends. Or wrestling. That's big out here in the Midwest. This man leads two lives and theft is a passion, a rush, a *need* that both sustains and destroys him. Call it compulsion. Call it a sickness. By any name there is no logic to his behavior, no sense or sensibility, and above all, though on the surface it may appear otherwise, his story is not a simple one of moral weakness.

These are the things I want to say. But I don't. The hour is nearly up and the nausea has grown stronger. Dizziness sets in. I let the class go early and find an old bar on the edge of town, the kind I like best, where it's always dark inside and the air smells sour from the night before. Nobody knows you here and doesn't care to and these are the people I am most comfortable with. There are no judgments. We share a common bond. I have earned my place beside them.

The nausea subsides with my third shot of Kessler's and soon the sweating and shaking stop. Those ants, though, they keep crawling because they want something else, something stronger that you can't find very easily in a small town like Vermillion, South Dakota. It's the meth, the speed. I ran out shortly after I arrived, and until now I don't think I realized just how badly I needed it. That I am strung out.

The next day, when I come to in my apartment, it starts all over again. The tremors. The fever. I know what will help, at least temporarily, but instead of reaching for the bottle I wrap myself in a blanket and weather it out. I am sick of being sick. I am tired of living a lie. Of waking up each morning and looking into the bathroom mirror at the bloodshot eyes and dark circles and thinking only of the next drink. The next line. The next fix. Anything to make me better.

Change or die, I tell myself.

The fever breaks early the following morning. They say the first forty-eight hours are the hardest, and I want to believe it's true, but I know they are only talking about the physical part of withdrawal. What's left, when the shaking and nausea subside, is far more insidious. It doesn't go away, either.

Not ever.

And that's the point I'm at. Here and now. Present time, looking back on that morning in South Dakota when the fever breaks, and I bathe. I dress. Then I take the rental car out onto the highway and drive, just drive. The sun is rising and I'm alone on this road.

Beyond the town there is nothing but open field. The land is flat and dusted white with snow. A wind blows like the wind at sea, rippling where the yellowed grasses still cling to the earth, shining with frost. There is no obstruction but the sky, and the sky is big, the sky is limitless. Out here there is no place to hide, and I park the car on the shoulder of the road. I get out and walk into the fields. The wind pulls at me, and I feel it in my ears, a ringing, a burning cold. Snow off the yellowed grasses blows down the neck of my jacket and dampens my chest and I look out across the fields, out across the sky, and in that vastness, as I close my eyes, I see my sons. Andy. Logan. Nate. I see their mother standing behind them. I see my own mother and father and the woman who will one day become my second wife. I see my brother-in-law. I see my niece. I see baby Katherine, I hear her cry, the first gasp of life.

I see my brother and sister, too. I see them clearly, and they are smiling at me. The wind grows stronger. I feel it cut into my skin. I feel it lifting me. I feel it carrying the three of us past the boundaries of our lives, and in our parting, when I open my eyes and the land rolls up toward me, endless and distant, breaking like a surf across the sky, I see my own story come to rest at a moment of beginning.

Acknowledgments

For believing in this book, I am indebted to my agent, Lisa Bankoff, and my editor, Claire Wachtel. I also need to thank those who have stood the true measure of friendship, Art Monterastelli, Manuel Palacios and Orlando Ramirez. I am likewise thankful for the love of my sons, Andrew, Logan and Nate, and their mother, Heidi, who endured too much. I am grateful to Amanda, Frank Ferro, Donna French, Maury Hirshberg, Kerry Kohn, Peter Schroeder and Jervey Tervelon. Special thanks go to Oakley Hall for his support from the very beginning. And to the woman without whom this book would never have been written, I credit my wife, Paula Priamos-Brown, for giving me a new life.

A Note on the Author

James Brown is the author of several novels including *Lucky Town* and *Final Performance*. He has received the Nelson Algren Award for Short Fiction, a National Endowment for the Arts Fellowship in fiction writing and a Chesterfield Film Writing Fellowship from Universal/Amblin Entertainment. His writing has been featured in the *Los Angeles Times Magazine*, the *New York Times Magazine* and the *New England Review*. He lives with his family in Lake Arrowhead, California.